Praise for
Thank God It's Monday!

"*Thank God It's Monday!* is an engrossing book that offers dynamic strategies on how to spark passion and enthusiasm in employees and create a workplace that the entire staff *wants* to come into every day. I have read hundreds of books on business strategy and how to increase productivity, but this is the first one that I will be buying for every one of my employees to read as well."

Ivan Misner, *The New York Times* best-selling author and founder of BNI, Business Networking International

"Roxanne motivates both men and women to cooperate in a manner that is engaging, brilliant, and inspiring."

John Gray, author of *Men Are from Mars, Women Are from Venus*

"I've always said that if our competitors got hold of Roxanne's information, we'd be in trouble. Fortunately, we found her first. Living this book will energize and engage your staff. Roxanne's systems work—especially during times like these."

Al Tubbs, CEO, Ohnward Bancshares, Inc., and past President of American Bankers Association

"Simple and profound, *Thank God It's Monday!* charges into the future, where employee fulfillment and customer service work hand-in-hand to create bottom-line results. Roxanne Emmerich has it right: Work can—and should be—fun. Be the force for creating trust and watch your company culture change."

Stephen M. R. Covey, author of *The Speed of Trust*

"In less than two years of using the *Thank God It's Monday!* approach, we not only met EVERY goal in ALL of our branches, but we exceeded many of our goals by 100 percent! Our entire organization acts like a team! I can't imagine any CEO who wouldn't want this for their organization."

Chad L. Hoffman, President & CEO, The Richwood Banking Company

"Roxanne Emmerich has shown companies all over the nation how to make people look forward to Monday. Her ideas reflect basic human values and understanding that can be rare in today's intense work life."

Gary Hoover, serial entrepreneur,
founder of Hoover's Business Information Service
and Hooversworld.com

"How do you motivate and inspire your team to work with purpose and passion? Put into practice the principles and actions found in *Thank God It's Monday!* Roxanne Emmerich has written a gem that will produce tremendous results for you and your organization!"

Chris Widener, columnist,
***SUCCESS* magazine**

"This book is brilliant. Buy it for everyone you know who needs to meet their goals NOW!"

Raymond Aaron,
***The New York Times* best-selling author**

"Within 30 days of our *Thank God It's Monday!* Kick-Butt Kick-Off™, we grew more than we had in the previous 10 years combined! The growth can only be described as a miracle and the profits were up 44%, and both have continued to soar from there."

Patti W. Steele, President & CEO,
First Volunteer Bank

"Life and business is vested in FRESH STARTS. Guided by this insightful work, every business will decide that Monday—each and every one of them—is a clear invitation to a fresh start. Get ready to add TGIM to your business attitude and strategic thinking."

Bob Danzig, former CEO, Hearst Newspapers,
author and Hall of Fame Speaker

"Roxanne Emmerich is a genius who communicates with authority and authenticity."

Dr. Nido Qubein, Board Executive Committee BB&T;
President, High Point University; Chairman,
Great Harvest Bread Co.

"Every employer and employee who is serious about being their best should read this book."

Bill Bachrach, Chairman & CEO of BAI,
author of *Values-Based Financial Planning*

"Our organization was a lazy underperformer until we discovered the *Thank God It's Monday!* process. Since our kick off, we've doubled in size and profits! The most important transformation, though, is that our people now expect to have a ball and to create success for themselves and the organization."

Archie R. McDonnell, Jr., President & CEO,
Citizens National Bank

"Roxanne's no-nonsense business approach, outstanding communication and leadership skills, and dedicated work ethic have undoubtedly made her one of most noted authors and inspirational business speakers in the country. Her book *Thank God's It's Monday!* epitomizes the very essence of these qualities and truly inspires a culture of positive change in the workplace."

Dan McGinty, President,
University of Wisconsin – River Falls Foundation

"We've moved from 3.3 services per household to 4.3 in 30 months. Loan growth was up $100 million in less than five months during the heart of a recession while we improved loan quality. Return on equity increased from 7.18% to 10.44% in a year. Net interest margin increased from 3.63% to 3.95% in a year with two major building projects factored in. And we had a breakthrough in spirit. The system works and we follow the system."

Jim Marcuccilli, CEO,
STAR Financial

"As a 30-year administrator with the University of St. Thomas College of Business, I have been aware for many years of Roxanne Emmerich's excellent national reputation as a premier consultant, teacher, advocate, and advisor to the finance and banking industry. Her most recent book, *Thank God It's Monday!*, provides a blueprint for powerful and positive changes in organizational culture that lead to major improvements in employee and customer satisfaction, which, in turn, lead to major improvements in the bottom line for any organization."

George E. Williams, Director of Operations and Administrative
Services, Opus College of Business, University of St. Thomas

"We paid for the full three-year program in the first month with a fee from a single client by following the new sales process we learned. We then went on to replicate those same results over and over again. But the real miracle is the transformation in our workplace culture."

J.J. Blake, President & CEO,
Peoples State Bank

"Since working with The Emmerich Group, we have reduced our turnover from 40% down to 2%."

Peter Morrison, President,
Elgin State Bank

"What a terrific title! And book! It's about a focus and practice that will shift a paradigm and experience. Roxanne knows that happy people are productive people; the most valuable asset in an organization is the people, and the highest leverage investment is in the people. She presents tested concepts, proven methods, and workable how-to's for transforming a company into one that is joyful, has meaning, contributes, produces results, and is a fun, cooperative, supportive environment. Can't wait for Monday..."

Terry Tillman, President, 22/7 Company,
Transformational Leadership Seminars

"Before Roxanne, we had lost direction. We knew we needed growth and a culture shift. Since joining The Emmerich Group, our deposits are up 22%, our customer satisfaction rating is 9.90 out of 10, and we are experiencing our most profitable year on record. This is the best investment we've ever made."

Jill D. Burnett, CEO,
Libertyville Savings Bank

"A valuable, idea-filled and superbly practical book on creating a great workplace."

Robin Sharma, #1 best-selling author of
The Monk Who Sold His Ferrari* and *The Greatness Guide

"Roxanne gives us so many memorable messages! The ideas she shares make sense immediately—you can see how they will produce positive changes in your business culture, changes that are sure to increase morale and your bottom line! *Thank God It's Monday!* is a fun and lively read full of gems."

Bobbi DePorter, President, Quantum Learning Network /
SuperCamp, and author of *Quantum Success*

Thank God It's Monday!

HOW TO CREATE A WORKPLACE
YOU AND YOUR CUSTOMERS LOVE

ROXANNE EMMERICH

Vice President, Publisher: Tim Moore
Associate Publisher and Director of Marketing: Amy Neidlinger
Editorial Assistant: Pamela Boland, Myesha Graham
Development Editor: Russ Hall
Operations Manager: Gina Kanouse
Digital Marketing Manager: Julie Phifer
Publicity Manager: Laura Czaja
Assistant Marketing Manager: Megan Colvin
Cover Designer: Chuti Prasertsith
Managing Editor: Kristy Hart
Project Editor: Chelsey Marti
Copy Editor: Water Crest Publishing
Proofreader: Language Logistics, LLC
Senior Indexer: Cheryl Lenser
Senior Compositor: Gloria Schurick
Manufacturing Buyer: Dan Uhrig

Publishing as FT Press
Upper Saddle River, New Jersey 07458

FT Press offers excellent discounts on this book when ordered in quantity for bulk purchases or special sales. For more information, please contact U.S. Corporate and Government Sales, 1-800-382-3419, corpsales@pearsontechgroup.com. For sales outside the U.S., please contact International Sales at international@pearson.com.

Company and product names mentioned herein are the trademarks or registered trademarks of their respective owners.

Kick-Butt Kick-Off, Energy Vampire, and Thank God It's Monday are trademarks of Leadership Avenue Press, LLC. Hoopla Team is a registered trademark of Leadership Avenue Press, LLC.

Printed in the United States of America

First Printing April 2009

ISBN-10: 0-13-815805-3
ISBN-13: 978-0-13-815805-7

Pearson Education LTD.
Pearson Education Australia PTY, Limited.
Pearson Education Singapore, Pte. Ltd.
Pearson Education North Asia, Ltd.
Pearson Education Canada, Ltd.
Pearson Educación de Mexico, S.A. de C.V.
Pearson Education—Japan
Pearson Education Malaysia, Pte. Ltd.

Library of Congress Cataloging-in-Publication Data

Emmerich, Roxanne, 1959-

Thank god it's monday! : how to create a workplace you and your customers love / Roxanne Emmerich.

p. cm.

ISBN 0-13-815805-3 (hardback : alk. paper) 1. Business. 2. Organizational effectiveness. 3. Employee morale. 4. Customer satisfaction. I. Title.

HD58.7.E436 2009

658.3'14—dc22

2008041938

To my readers who have decided to live a life of significance and make your work meaningful for yourself and others. You deserve to have it all.

And to my kids who light up my life—may your path have heart and your contributions be massive.

Contents

Contents

Acknowledgments

Khalil Gibran said, "Work is love made visible." This book is a work of love and it came from the many cheerleaders, coaches, teachers, advisors, friends, and family who were tireless in making sure this work got out there in a big way and that this book happened.

I'd like to start by thanking my clients—those leaders who saw an even bigger possibility for your organization and your team and decided to go for it. And thank you to all the receptionists, middle managers, sales people, and other people from throughout the organizations who said, "I'm committed to getting my leadership team engaged in this." Leadership is not a position but a way of being and you were the leaders in transforming your organizations. You have earned your legacy.

The line between client and friend has become fuzzy as I think it should. Although the list of client-friends has become long, there are a few who have been a standout for this book and put in hours to read, give ideas, and push for this to happen. They were the ones who requested I write this book so it would be available to make their customers more successful. Special thanks goes to Archie McDonnell, Jr., J.J. Blake, David Barr, Dale Hopper, Patti Steele, Chad Hoffman, Mark Abate, Pete Morrison, and Mike Hannley who read and gave input to the book and served as a support team for this work.

Stewart Emery lit up when he heard of this project. Much appreciation for the stand you've taken to make this book happen and to connect me with the publishing team at Pearson.

Thanks go to the publishing team at Pearson who helped make this book a reality: Russ Hall, Tim Moore, Amy Neidlinger, Megan Colvin, Chelsey Marti, and Gloria Schurick.

There are many dear friends and colleagues who have been my inspiration and teachers on this project—too many to mention. Special thank yous to those who in some way assisted in making this book a reality through reading, coaching, or sharing brilliance or sweat; Ford Saeks, Stephanie Wolf, Pete Bissonette, Mary Marcdante, Sam Horn, C. Leslie Charles, Dianna Booher, Greg Link, Dan Janal, Joan Emery, Bobbie DePorter, David Garfinkel, Dale McGowen, Joyce Belle, David Lieber, Mark Mayfield, and Marci Shimoff.

Thank you to the team at The Emmerich Group as well as our extended team. You have given of your spirit to do your work with vision—much gratitude for your commitment to transforming lives and businesses. You have been the wind beneath my wings.

Thanks to mom and to my dad who recently passed. You taught me how to care with all my heart. That, I have discovered, matters more than anything.

And special thanks to my children. What we lost in time together while I traveled we made up for with a playful spirit and a love for living life full on. Thank you for sharing me with your world and allowing me to be a raving fan at thousands, (did I say thousands? Yes, I think I did) of soccer games, baseball games, karate matches, choir concerts, swim meets, band concerts, and kitchen rapping contests—you made being a mom as wonderful and exciting as it could ever be. Thanks Brandon, Casey, Steph, and Spencer and our exchange student children Michael, Jon, and Hiroya. You rock my world and keep my playful spirit alive.

And then there is my husband, David. You made me belly laugh the first time I met you and have worked tirelessly to make sure I kept laughing every day since then while you showered me with love. You've made this ride a fun one.

Meet
Roxanne Emmerich

Roxanne Emmerich has consulted with half of the nation's top 1% performing financial institutions as well as hundreds of other business leaders. Her book, *Profit-Growth Banking*, has been called "the bible of successful business."

A 20-year management consultant and three-time Entrepreneur of the Year winner, Roxanne has proven that companies grow when their people grow. Her new book, *Thank God It's Monday!*, outlines a system for bringing profits and fun to business. She shows how to create a "Thank God It's Monday" workplace with employees on fire and a bottom line that proves it. She uses her "Kick-Butt Kick-Off" strategy to create immediate culture shifts and achieve tangible results.

A member of the National Speakers Hall of Fame, she is noted by *Sales and Marketing Management* magazine as one of the most requested speakers for instilling a "bring it on" attitude. She has written hundreds of articles and is frequently interviewed by national media for practical business insights.

A distinguished alum of the University of Wisconsin, Roxanne served as a key advisor to former Wisconsin Governor Tommy Thompson and as Editor-In-Chief of *Extraordinary Banker* magazine. She is also the founder of "Permission to Be Extraordinary Summit," an executive breakthrough program run by her company, The Emmerich Group.

Roxanne resides in Minneapolis with her husband and children.

www.EmmerichGroup.com

introduction

"Oh, great you say. A book about having fun at work. Whoop-de-rah."

I've heard it all by now. Serious business people think that means going around with a lot of happy talk while painting smiley faces on everything. They couldn't be more wrong.

In point of fact, fun is a byproduct of the approach I advocate. What you're really after is to grow the business by being more efficient at what you do and being linked with your customers at a human and meaningful level, and that all can happen when you have a more motivated workplace. This means you need to have a workplace people enjoy, including your customers. Especially your customers.

This is a time-tested approach that many, many companies have used to get very real, surprisingly super-sized results. As a consultant I have had the privilege to partner in creating profound change for hundreds of companies. We repeatedly see significant shifts in growth and profits within six months! Many businesses double profits and size within three years. You can see a large sampling of testimonials at the front of the book.

> This is a time-tested approach that many, many companies have used to get very real, surprisingly super-sized results.

This predictable, repeatable process really works. It's all I do, which makes me the right person to share this process and the real-life stories of people and businesses that have embraced it.

In the book, you'll hear a lot of stories. I've changed the names to protect the guilty as well as the innocent. But the stories are all about real people. You may recognize some of the characters from where you work, the good as well as the bad. Stories work better than my showing you a lot of pie charts and graphs because the secret is all about people—you and your people and the people with whom you connect on a daily basis.

The most exciting part is that positive, measurable changes that really matter can begin in a single day. Mind you, it's going to take some diligent follow-up as you roll out new standards and refresh your vision. But the best way for you to understand this is to read on.

—Roxanne Emmerich

PART I

A Problem...
or an Opportunity

chapter one

"Thank God It's *Monday*"

"Work and play are words used to describe the same thing under differing conditions."

—Mark Twain

Anyone who has ever taken a car trip with a medium to large family has experienced (or at least heard of) that moment when Mom or Dad has to turn and say, "Don't make me stop this car and come back there."

Well, why not? For starters, it's raining so hard outside that the wipers can't quite keep up, and the driver, Dad, can barely see—he couldn't get to sleep after pouring over maps with too many cups of coffee until way past midnight. Mom is just starting to imagine she left the backdoor unlocked, forgot to stop the mail, and...did she leave the oven on? The air in the vehicle feels and smells stuffy, even though the air conditioner is set higher than it should be. Tensions have been mounting for some time. Someone wants to go to a bathroom, even though they had just left one 20 minutes ago. Angie is lobbying for the highway to make time, while Robbie wants to take the back roads and visit the giant ball of string. Little Kelsie is in full gear whine, "I didn't want to go on this stupid trip in the first place—I wanted to stay home with my friends. Waaa, waaa, waaa."

Now, imagine that's not the family traveling on a holiday, but it is a business going about its daily course of trying to keep afloat in as difficult and competitive marketplace as has ever existed.

In a way, any business is a lot like a family. Psychologists like to talk about dysfunctional families—without whom television sitcoms would be at a loss for subject matter—and fully functional families, the latter being an ideal that is seemingly never entirely realized. You have probably walked into a bank or restaurant or department store and thought, "Yep. Dysfunctional." The employees are not getting along, and you're the recipient of all the toxic venom you can endure in the time you're there; next you realize they serve their attitude "to go" because it stays with you for some time after you leave.

> You have probably walked into a bank or restaurant or department store and thought, "Yep. Dysfunctional."

However, if you've been paying attention, you've also walked into other businesses where the people seem to genuinely enjoy each other's presence. They are happy, and it shows in the quality of their work, and this infuses your experience as a customer.

Believe it or not, there actually *are* places where people wake up after a weekend, glance at the clock, and say, "**Thank God It's Monday**." They are eager to get back to work. Work is a "get to go to" place, not an "I have to deal with" place.

It is the kind of workplace you, no doubt, would like to have. It's actually about more than this. It is the kind that you need to have if your company is to thrive and if you, as a person, want to feed your soul and replenish your spirit so that you really get to live life instead of just tolerate it.

Now, if you are like most people, you can honestly say you have never worked in a motivated environment. You don't even think it's possible, and you're already thinking "yeah, right" about the whole concept of ANYBODY saying, "**Thank God It's Monday**." Or you're thinking, "I gotta bail from this place. My place is dysfunctional." Of course, you may have bailed from the last workplace for the same reason. And what did it get you? Out of the frying pan into the fire, maybe?

6

If you're an executive, you've probably heard the statistics and stories that link workplace aliveness to bottom line impact. A Gallup study shows that for the average company, for every $10,000 of payroll, $3,400 is factored in for lost productivity flowing from disengaged employee factors in the workplace. You know you can no longer afford disengaged employees.

> Believe it or not, there actually are places where people wake up after a weekend, glance at the clock, and say, "Thank God It's *Monday.*"

If you're a manager, you know how much of your time is spent dealing with what seems to you to be dysfunctional behaviors or "problem" employees.

If you are any person within the organization, you know how much your energy is drained by those who don't want to play the big game, by the drama queens and kings, and assorted other crazy-making stuff you now just tolerate because you don't see any another choice. You also know it hurts your psyche, your physical body feels the stress, and you have shut down to protect yourself.

So, what can you do? First, do great "**Thank God It's *Monday***" workplaces really exist? Yes. Absolutely. Unequivocally. And before they were great, most were quite awful.

Okay, so now you may be thinking, "Sure, they happen 'out there,' but can we ever really get our organization to come alive? Our people don't just have issues—their issues have issues. We have so far to go. I really think if there is ever a place where it couldn't happen, this would be the place."

If you're thinking like this, you're not alone. In fact, welcome to the majority. Well, you can turn it around and find yourself loving your work and creating massive results while you're at it.

Don't believe me? Well, tag along for a bit.

OK—Let's Be Real

You've probably noticed that no organization came alive because an executive gave the order to "Have fun NOW."

That's not what I'm talking about here, although, heaven help us, some bosses have tried that. What I want you to experience, to discover, is a way to rock your workplace into becoming a more enjoyable place for everyone to be, a place that creates wonderful results, celebrates successes, and creates the mindsets and skills so that people make themselves great and others greater, instead of tearing each other down—too often the norm in most workplaces. You'll notice a profound difference, and your customers will, too. And the business and profits will grow because of it.

It's not as easy as giving an order or waving a magic wand. But it is doable and has been done in many businesses already, and it can change not only your workplace but also your life.

Let's take a look at a few businesses and see just how the heck they do it. The message here is relevant whether you are a CEO or a front-line employee.

We could poke our noses into a lot of businesses, restaurants, banks, and stores, but let's push our luck in the next chapter and go into the kind of service center where you expect to have a junkyard dog of an experience.

chapter two

There Really ARE Good Places to Work

"The good life, as I conceive it, is a happy life. I do not mean that if you are good you will be happy; I mean that if you are happy you will be good."

—Bertrand Russell

Sara Grimes, a 32-year-old working single mother of two, is driving along in her Honda Civic near a road construction stretch in Austin, Texas, and "POW"—a rock flies off a dump truck, and she suddenly has a giant spider web on her windshield. Never a fun moment. Worse, she certainly can't call her ex-husband, who is two child support payments behind as it is.

She is on her own. She has the weekday off to get ready for a trip, but time is an issue since she has to pick up Bryce after soccer practice and Alice from a harp lesson. So she goes home to check the yellow pages and look up locations for a repair spot near her. She even gets on the Internet to check reviews for a bunch of the places.

Some are just plain scary.

One reviewer describes the car window repair shop she visited as being in a junkyard, complete with a pit bull. The reviewer says she sat in her car, too scared to go inside, and finally drove away. Now, just about a nervous wreck and already thinking this is going to cost at least $600 or more (a lot more if she goes to a dealership), Sara calls her friend Mariah, who tells Sara to be sure to include Longhorn Glass in her search.

Sara gets back on the Internet and all, I mean *all*, of the reviews for Longhorn Glass are positive, almost too good to be true. She calls Longhorn Glass and gets a friendly voice, a quick quote, and the best price, less than a quarter of what she feared she might have to pay. So she fires up her hurting Honda and heads for the place. It's in a tiny strip mall across I-35 from the University of Texas campus. The surrounding setting is rough to the eye, but a line of cars is pulled up to the garage doors. She hesitates but pulls in anyway.

Inside there is nothing fancy, but the initial sensation she gets is palpable, overwhelming, and positive. Just like the reviews. She gets a genuine and understanding smile from the woman behind the desk, who remembers Sara from her call. "The Honda Civic. Right?" She gets Sara's keys and tells her that she'll be back on the street in 45 minutes. Sara sits down and looks around while she waits. There are signs and posters about teamwork, attitude, and determination. One sign says, "We want you to either come in with a smile or leave with one." The biggest sign of all, covering much of the wall behind the counter, says, "It is the job of every Longhorn Glass employee to excel at acquiring and retaining customers by meeting their individual needs with honesty, courtesy, and a commitment to customer satisfaction."

Well, we've all seen signs like that—they're kind of standard fair these days and tend to engender more cynicism than customer confidence or satisfaction.

Now here's the really amazing part. For the short time Sara is there, she actually sees that they not only talk the talk, but they walk the walk. Everyone, and I do mean everyone, seems to enjoy working with each other. Their chatter with each other and with Sara is friendly and interested. The handyman comes through, and he's grinning and kidding around as he picks up and sweeps, keeping the place as tidy as a place that repairs windows can be. The guy putting in her new windshield comes in to ask Sara where she wants her stickers placed. Even when Sara leaves, they all let her know they've all had a better day because she was a part of it. She glances at the calendar on the way out and realizes, gadzooks, today is really Monday.

Incredible? But possible. A light bulb flashes on in Sara's head, and for the first time she starts to toy with the idea, "Why can't the place I work be more like this?"

Sara's mind begins to embrace the idea that if a place on the tougher side of the highway that fixes broken car windows can be a great place to be, then maybe working where she works could be fun. Maybe somehow she could do something to help make that happen. If the customers felt the way she had felt at Longhorn Glass, well then, business may just pick up as a result. That would be good for everyone. Sara could distantly recall that succeeding always felt like more fun than failing!

> A light bulb flashes on in Sara's head, and for the first time she starts to toy with the idea, "Why can't the place I work be more like this?"

With her eyes wide open to the possibility, Sara Grimes continued to look around at businesses that knew how to have fun and at others that didn't. The fun ones seemed to be more successful, too.

* * *

The next day, heading for a routine visit to the corporate offices, she parked the Honda in long-term parking and headed for the Southwest gates at Austin-Bergstrom International Airport. Getting through security looked like it was going to be a breeze, and she could hear and see a seriously good Western Americana group playing live music on the other side of the checkpoint. Sara just loved the sound of good music—and the accompanying fragrant aroma of authentic Texas barbecue bordered on seductive as her taste buds came alive in response. Well, it was close enough to lunch time and a while before flight time so…. This place always felt way better than most every other airport she had ever been to, and she had been to more than a few. It put her in a better mood about travel.

As Sara got settled on her Southwest Airlines flight, one of the flight attendants announced, "We'll be dimming the lights in the cabin. Pushing the light-bulb button will turn on your reading light. However, pushing the flight-attendant button will not turn on your flight attendant." Then she heard from the pilot, "Weather at our destination is 72 degrees with some broken clouds, but we'll try to have them fixed before we arrive. Thank you, and remember, nobody loves you, or your money, more than Southwest Airlines." Then from another flight attendant, "Your seat cushions can be used for flotation, and in the unlikely event of an emergency water landing, please paddle to shore and take them with our compliments."

The atmosphere on such a flight reflected the madcap willingness to have a little fun. People got up from their seats and roamed to talk to other passengers. It felt like a party in the sky.

All she had to do for a comparison and contrast was to recall some flights on other domestic airlines where she had witnessed employees snapping at each other, giving her surly looks, or going about their jobs with the mechanical dullness of the uninspired. She asked herself for which airline would she rather work? On which one would she rather fly? And this airline wasn't alone. She had heard that Virgin Airlines is an equally fun airline to fly. As Sir Richard Branson tells it, "We have more experience than our name would suggest." She remembered reading about Branson's determination to "do it" (whatever "it" was) and to make sure the doing of it was fun. He maintained that without the fun quotient, the chances of success in any undertaking were severely diminished, even obliterated.

Arriving a day early for her business meeting and eager to work off the effects of the time zone change from Austin to Orange County,

Sara drove around and eventually ended up at one of Southern California's finest shopping malls—Fashion Island Newport Beach. Walking into one of the biggest shopping malls she'd ever seen, Sara was so overwhelmed she decided to not shop but just to explore during this visit. She had been keeping a log of workplaces that seemed fun and those that didn't. So far, one side of the ledger had far more entries than the fun side. But she had hope. At a blazing speed, she poked her nose into about 50 stores in about an hour.

It didn't take her long to notice that there seemed to be an unwritten script that was followed in every store. She'd walk in, and a salesperson would say, without fail, "Can I help you?" to which she replied, "No, just looking." Apparently relieved that Sara had gotten her line right, the salesperson would retreat, preparing for the next entrance, the next exchange of lines—and the next, and the next— until at last each salesclerk could go home, eat dinner, watch television, go to sleep, wake up....

Then, at one store, the experience was different. A clerk smiled at her, seemed genuinely glad she was there, and said, *"Stay right there."*

She froze and experienced mixed expectations. Had the clerk mistaken her for the mug shot of their last shoplifter? The clerk came back with a sweater, draped it over her shoulders, and gently guided her to a mirror and said, "Look what this sweater does to your eyes! You'd have to carry a baseball bat to beat away the men."

Sara asked the only reasonable question, "How much?"

When she left the store, her large bag contained a number of other items, including gifts for her kids she had also willingly added to her purchase. What made the difference wasn't some con artist's polished pitch, but the real enthusiasm of a person who does more than go through the motions of a job. This is a person who looks forward to coming to work each day and interacting with others. Most people spend their entire lives in unquestioned routines, never hearing the calling of how great they could be if only they refocused on making a profound difference through their work—no matter what they do.

You might even feel some guilt yourself about all the ways you conform each day to what you think your work "gig" is. In fact, it may seem like almost every person around you also conforms to what others expect as the norm without thinking about how to be extraordinary and to give powerful and profound service.

> Most people spend their entire lives in unquestioned routines, never hearing the calling of how great they could be if only they refocused on making a profound difference through their work.

In your years of shopping for products or using services, you can no doubt recall numerous comparative moments when the experience was good, bad, or ugly. You've met the clerk too busy stocking shelves to let you near what you want, and you have been surprised by the bank teller with sparkling, eager eyes who seemed genuinely glad to see you. So, you have some points of comparison to know whether where you work is a good place.

The point is, there really are good places to work and, as you can affirm, also bad places. What do you want your workplace to be like? And what can you do to make it a "**Thank God It's Monday**" kind of place?

Try this:

- Keep track in the next 10 businesses you enter. Do the employees seem to get along? Are they happy? Is your experience positive or negative as a result of the way people act and feel?

- As you visit stores and businesses, seek to determine if each is a good place to work. What would you change if you were CEO there?

- Explore the Internet and watch for the qualities that bloggers, reviewers, and customers use to describe a positive or negative experience.

- Measure where you work by the best and worst of what you have seen elsewhere. How does your workplace measure up?

chapter three

But I've Got a Business to Run

"Each day, and the living of it, has to be a conscious creation in which discipline and order are relieved with some play and pure foolishness."

—May Satton

Roger Milford took a deep breath and caught the salty scent of the nearby sea mingled with chlorine and coconut suntan lotion as he headed around the oversized, liver-shaped pool. The fronds of palm trees swayed in the breeze, and high above a gull dipped and turned in the cloudless blue of the sky. His eyes flicked around, summing up the people: sunburned vacationers, honeymooners, and a handful of wild middle-aged crazies reliving spring break madnesses of days gone by.

He stopped abruptly when he saw Kathy Pillshard taking the tiny umbrella out of her piña colada at a table beside the pool bar. They were both CEOs of similar-sized banking companies on opposite coasts. They didn't compete and kept an eye on how each other was doing. He first met her when they shared a cab to the airport after a trade show in Phoenix years ago. He'd initially been surprised to learn she had a two-finger whistle of which any construction worker would be proud. It had certainly landed them a cab. He had heard her present at the show, so he knew her to be a pretty shrewd cookie as well. He hadn't seen her since a trade show two years ago.

"Good heavens, Kathy. What are you doing here in Cancun?"

"About anyone with a passport can come down here, Roger."

"I'll bet you're celebrating. I read all about your outfit embarrassing the rest of us with your growth. Up 30 percent or something, weren't you?" Roger caught himself holding in his stomach beneath his Hawaiian shirt and let himself relax. He carried the confident extra few pounds of someone who had lived well and always been assertive. But a sea of change in his business world had put a cautious dent in any of the former overconfidence he had once displayed.

"Thirty-two," she said. He was pretty sure he caught her suppressing the outright grin he expected by lifting her glass and taking a sip.

"I don't know how you did it. I had to push harder than ever to get a measly three percent growth. These have been a couple of tough years. I read where you turned around your outfit by everyone having fun at work. I figured that was a lot of fluff for the trade journal."

"No fluff, Roger. That's exactly how we did it. Together. It's not as simple as just having fun. It was an extreme makeover of our whole culture, into a better one, where we enjoy being around each other and feel more fulfilled. Plus, we get the kind of results you seem to be drooling about."

Roger gave a huff. He wasn't buying it. Still, although his laptop and a briefcase full of paperwork may be waiting for him in his room, he kept listening. Kathy had always been someone with whom he could have candid discussions. More than once he'd been glad they were on opposite coasts and didn't compete. And more than once he had thought she could look inside him like he was a spreadsheet.

"Believe the 32 percent, then, Roger. Those are numbers you can't dispute."

"Well, the article I read said you'd turned everything around in a day. I found that a tall glass to drink from."

"You're right. That paints a picture that's not quite complete. It did all start in a day. We noticed some change immediately. But there's also a lot of follow-up, a careful and deliberate system of roll-outs that kept us transforming after that."

"A day? What can you do in a day?"

"A lot, as it turns out." She waved to a chair, and Roger sat down. "That day was just the beginning. The top managers and I spent time beforehand learning a system and process for the makeover of our culture. Then, in an evening session, we had all the employees come together where in a 'kick-off' session, we created a vision for them of what being extraordinary would look like, and we got the whole group to commit to making it happen, to how we would treat our customers and each other. Then there's all that follow-up I mentioned, all required if any change is going to be sustained."

> It did all start in a day. We noticed some change immediately. But there's also a lot of follow-up, a careful and deliberate system of roll-outs that kept us transforming after that.

"All so work could be more enjoyable? Well, you may have the luxury of time for that sort of thing, but I have a business to run."

"Sounds like it was a hard run for you, and with only a three percent gain to show for it."

"I guess you do have some cause to celebrate."

"Truth is, Roger, you're right about celebrating. I'm down here with a group of our front-line employees. They're being rewarded for breakthrough results, so I got to come with them. You see, I've improved a lot, too."

"A vacation with employees. I came here to get away from mine."

"There, in a nutshell, you have the key difference, Roger."

"Well, maybe I will look into whatever you did. I can't argue with that kind of success."

"Here come my vacation mates." Kathy waved at a group across the pool coming around their way. "Tell you what. Why don't you ask one of them? Get their version. You remember Kevin, my personal assistant. You've talked to him before on the phone."

"That festering boil. I thought you were going to have to fire him. I've rarely had anyone be so rude to me."

"Turns out he was a keeper once we showed him how to ignite a passion for customer results. It's about coming from a place of caring and giving."

"This all sounds too touchy-feely for me."

"Thirty-two percent, Roger. How touchy-feely is that?"

"Okay, I'll talk to Kevin. But if he's anything like before, he's going into the pool."

THE VALUE PROPOSITION

The approach I'm encouraging you to consider is more than just about "fun," although that's clearly part of it. The fun is actually a consequence of committing to exceptional outcomes and to treating each other and customers with respect and warmth. It's really about building a results-focused company culture that everyone will notice and talk about. When done correctly, and that means with a thorough follow-up and regular maintenance, it will make your workplace more enjoyable and, because of that, more productive. The best aspects of the approach include the following:

1. Measurable results that happen on the first day in culture and performance.

> 2. A buzz your customers create about how great it is to be your customer—to the extent they act as advocates for you to their friends. Your business will grow.
>
> 3. The benefits even extend into the homes and lives of you and your employees. Your kids will say, "What happened to you? Can you do more of it?"

Kevin got a beer from the bar and sat down at the table while Kathy went to join the others in a game of water volleyball in the pool.

"Roger, I think I probably owe you an overdue apology."

Roger shook the extended hand. "How's that?"

"Oh, I have a good idea how I could be back then. When Kathy brought in a consultant for the kick-off day that would orchestrate the company's change process, I was the one who murmured, 'Let's string her up.' But I couldn't have been more wrong, not that I went gentle into that good night. Truth is, I was quite bitter back then. My marriage was rocky, my finances were a mess, and I was a world-class grump, especially at work. Any other company would have let me go."

"But Kathy kept you. Why?"

"I was spotted right away as one of the people on the fence. I thought the whole thing was one more desperate attempt to grab the 'flavor of the month' from the world of business self-improvement. I kicked and fussed, and in the follow-up process even got caught being rude to a mystery shopper. Anyway, I ended up having this sit-down talk with Kathy where I had to decide one way or the other whether I was going to commit to being accountable for my actions, to communicating constructively, to being part of making a difference. I talked it over with my wife, and that was the start of us getting along better, too. It was the first open and honest talk I'd had with her in a long time."

"All this from Kathy's buying into making the workplace more enjoyable?"

"Well, it was the whole thing. Once I decided that 'I can do it,' I started actually to have more fun at work. I ended up on a Hoopla Team®. That's a crew that keeps things going by bringing out fresh initiatives that get measured and celebrated. You know, kind of like when you're at the gym and you're working out, and you realize you aren't feeling any positive burn in a muscle set, so you do a different exercise until that tightens up."

It had been a long while since Roger had the kind of time that allowed him to darken a gym door, but he figured Kevin spent more time working out than at the library.

"I even went to a boot camp, which sounded awful but turned out to be a really good experience." Kevin took a drink from his beer that finished it. He put the bottle down and glanced to where the others were splashing at their sport. "Mind you, I was a real foot-dragger in the early going, but once I got on board, I was genuinely sorry I hadn't embraced all this from the beginning. You can't even begin to imagine the word-of-mouth buzz that began after the kick-off. The whole community was talking about how different our company was now, and our clients began turning up with their friends."

> The whole community was talking about how different our company was now, and our clients began turning up with their friends.

"My wife could tell you the same story. We not only weathered our rough patch, but things are better than ever between us now. I guess when you make the effort to get along with people and be a part of making things better, results happen at home, too."

"It sounds like a miracle to me." Roger didn't shake his head, but he started to think about that pile of work upstairs that wasn't going to take care of itself.

"Well, it turned out to be one for me. It takes work. But now it doesn't feel so much like work. It mostly feels like fun. I'm working harder than ever, but I'm having a hoot. I'd been counting off the months until retirement, and now I think they're going to have to push me out of there when that time comes." Kevin rose and tugged his T-shirt off his disgustingly fit torso. "And now, if you'll please excuse me, I've got some volleyball to play."

Roger watched them. A boss and her employees playing side by side. What a concept. Well, that would never happen at his company. But maybe Kathy was right about that. Maybe that was the problem. He could have gone to his room, but he stayed to watch them a while. They sure did seem to know how to have fun.

Try this:

- Walk around your business as if you are a customer seeing it for the first time. Does it make you want to bring all your appropriate business to this business, or do you feel employee tensions and lack of professionalism that would cause you to doubt your desire to do any business?

- Identify the areas that are most in need of improvement—certain customer service moments of truth like how your phones are answered, how you greet visitors, the speed with which things are done, the accuracy of transactions, and any other key moments when customers form an impression of you.

- Ask yourself, "What can I do immediately to fix any areas needing adjustment?" Leadership is not a position but a way of being, so take charge of whatever you can. Greet with great warmth. Clean up areas that are left a mess. Find a way to be an example of someone who cares and truly contributes.

- Be a lead in responding with a "How CAN we?" mindset as opportunities present themselves. When your teammates tell you why they can't do something (hit a deadline, meet a sales goal, or get a major account), respond by asking, "How CAN you?" Repeat that with every new objection until your teammates understand that you are taking a stand for them to be strong, committed, and powerful in getting great results.

chapter four

Who Can Take Action—Everyone!

"Lead, follow, or get out of the way."

—Thomas Paine

Now, you may be thinking that it's okay to talk about making the workplace a more enjoyable environment, but how can you do that when you're not the CEO or for that matter, when you *are* the CEO. We'll take a look at having a vision in a bit, but for now let's consider the whole point of leadership and why it can exist anywhere.

Here's the thing. Leadership is not a position—it's a way of being. It's about being determined to make big things happen regardless of your position. In sports, someone like Michael Jordan showed that the leader wasn't the one sitting on the bench in the pinstripe suit, but it was a player who worked harder in practices, put more effort into every game, elevated the level of his teammates, and helped them all remember that basketball is a game, and you can have fun playing, particularly if you are winning a lot.

> Leadership is not a position—it's a way of being. It's about being determined to make big things happen regardless of your position.

Take Pearl Samuels, who took a position as a receptionist and turned a company around. She showed up with hair the color and texture of corn silk tossing in the wind and with a round farm girl freshness to her, as if she would not be unfamiliar with how to plow a field or bail hay. She had brought some of that work ethic from the fields of Iowa with her, and though she looked like someone who liked her morning doughnut, she was rarely seen when she was not doing something and doing it better than it had ever been done. What she didn't know she was quick to learn, and within weeks she was blowing away the incoming callers with her zest for life. Customers started to buy more and send their friends to do business with that company.

Pearl's Dad had been a Navy officer, and perhaps that, in part, was why her desk was always as trim and clear as the deck of an aircraft carrier. She didn't put things into piles to be done later. They left her hands and were wafted as if magically to the right places, often in multi-task fashion while she fielded incoming calls and visitors to the lobby, which, by the way, sported fresh flowers each Monday by her doing. As soon as she caught on to how orders were routed, placed, and handled, she saw apparent redundancies that could be eliminated. She stepped in, diplomatically, and helped fix that when not on the phone. Orders continued to increase, and the workload was cut in half because of the more efficient system she had helped create.

A month into the job, she spotted three employees with "attitude." She, on her own time, talked to each one separately and persuaded them to bring their whole heart into the workplace because the customers expect that. She let them know the impact of their behavior on her and how they could specifically do things differently. They changed.

One day, a big deal came in the door, and she handled the greeting so well that the prospect made a large purchase and raved to all her friends, also huge prospects, about how well she had been taken care of. More deals like that came flying in the door. Pearl realized there was no follow-up plan for new customers, so she helped devise, develop, and implement a plan for keeping track of calls and for sending gifts to the clients. Again, customers raved and sent their friends.

When a morale issue developed due to jealousy, Pearl talked to each person and offered them good advice and encouraged them to stop sulking and to talk through the issue before it destroyed working relationships. Within a few years, she was running the place. People who "step up to the plate," who see an opportunity to make an impact and seize it are infinitely promotable AND endlessly valuable.

How can you be more like Pearl? Notice, she accomplished massive results without a position of authority by recognizing opportunities, being completely accountable for the results of the company, and without being controlling, heavy-handed, or neurotic; she brought along others to also get great results.

> People who "step up to the plate," who see an opportunity to make an impact and seize it are infinitely promotable AND endlessly valuable.

Try this:

- List three things that, if you were in charge, you would change.
- Set about doing all you can to change those things— enrolling others to your ideas, getting necessary approvals, lining up a budget, or coaching others around you to go "get it." And watch the magic happen.

PART II

Rock Your World:
Initiating Change

chapter five

Shifting a Company's Gears: The Unreasonable Premise

"All truth passes through three stages. First, it is ridiculed. Second, it is violently opposed. Third, it is accepted as being self-evident."

—Arthur Schopenhauer

Kathy Pillshard got to Smith & Wollensky's at 11:15 before the big lunch crowd push had a chance to arrive. She hadn't lived in Manhattan for several years but still knew the way to her favorite steakhouse. As the door closed behind her, she left the street noise of cabs honking and buses grinding out on Third Avenue. Inside, the ambiance shifted to tastefully quiet. She was led to a table in the far corner where Roger Milford sat with a cup of coffee and *The Wall Street Journal* in front of him.

He swept the paper to an empty chair and stood while she was seated. When he sat again, Kathy took in the drawn lines of his face and a new wrinkle or two on his brow. "You must be really curious to spring for porterhouses here," she said.

"It's been six months since I bumped into you at Cancun, and I thought since we were both here in the city for a trade show, you might let me pick your brain about what worked so well for you."

The waiter came, and they placed their orders. Kathy smiled to herself. Roger sure looked like the boy who stood on the burning deck. In the years she'd known him, he had always been a proud and assertive man. It must have taken every shred of humility he could muster to come to her for help and advice.

As the waiter walked away, she asked, "So, how have things been going with your company since I last saw you?"

"Not good. I told you we'd downsized and trimmed the budget to the bone. But any growth is slipping away. I don't know what to do. We're a sinking ship with nothing left to throw overboard."

Kathy could have reminded him she had advised against the path he'd taken, but they had been friends too long for rubbing salt in wounds—too long to mention her company was still making gains while his was close to flat-lining. "What do you want to know, Roger?"

"Well, the whole thing, if it's something you can share. How it starts, the steps, and, well, the whole process."

"Well, first off I've got to tell you, Roger, that if 10 companies took this approach, there might be 10 different versions, but I can give you the high points. It all started when I paid attention to our suggestion box."

> **If 10 companies took this approach, there might be 10 different versions, but I can give you the high points.**

"Really."

"Yeah, really."

Their salads arrived, and Kathy picked up her salad fork. "I got a suggestion note from a front-line worker at a Texas branch, Sara Grimes. She asked if we couldn't make our company a place where we all loved to work, where we had more fun and get results, too. I know what you're probably thinking. Does that mean computer games on company machines, nap times, parties each day? Well, no, though we do celebrate a good bit."

She waited until they'd finished their salads and the steaks had arrived—with a baked a potato for him and a selection of seasonal vegetables for her. She cut into her steak, just the right shade of pink.

"I had Sara fly in and talk to me at my office about her suggestion, and she told me she'd been to other businesses where everyone seemed to enjoy being around each other more. She'd changed dry cleaners when a friend told her about the one she used where people not only seemed to enjoy each other, but also welcomed every customer in a way that had them feeling special and cared for. They would watch the people park, run for their clothes, and when they walked in the door, the employees would smile and call out, 'Mr. Anderson, I have your dry cleaning ready for you right here.' Is your dry cleaner like that? Mine wasn't."

"So I asked around myself, found one near me that everyone said was run like Sara's, where you feel more like a family member than a customer, and I switched. I told myself that if customers were advocating a place and it was gaining business because of it, and the people got along better too, then this was something I should look into."

"Anyone can do this?" Roger asked. She envied the way he went at his baked potato covered in sour cream and chives. She knew she'd be hitting the hotel gym for a treadmill run herself after this steak. But it was worth it.

"I suppose anyone could. We hired a consultant to get an outside set of eyes helping us, and we got a lot of help for our program. To be honest, a lot of what was shared wasn't earth-shatteringly new to me.

> I told myself if customers were advocating a place and it was gaining business because of it, while the people got along better too, then this was something I should look into.

It was more about taking all the complex things that we make too hard and making them instead into a simple step-by-step process. You've heard the expression, 'I think, therefore I complicate.' Well, we were good at that! So, from customer service strategies and execution, to how we hire, to how we do morning huddles and quarterly celebrations, quarterly reviews, you name it—all these things we made simple, where the focus became getting better results. And work became enjoyable—loads of fun, actually. That's what it's about. Perhaps it sounds too simple to work, but when we put it all together, well, the results speak for themselves."

Roger raised a bite of steak to his mouth and nodded for her to go on.

"We scheduled a kick-off meeting, which is a one-day event for all employees. This was the real beginning; although for a few weeks before the event, I gathered everyone from upper management together into a leadership team, and we put our heads together to be sure we had a clear picture of a vision for how we wanted the company to be and the values we held that would drive the change. Most of us thought we already knew all this, but our eyes were opened during what turned out to be quite candid talks—for example, about how a lot of the time it seemed like we were running an adult daycare center rather than the business we were actually in. This had to change. I wanted to know I had the commitment from each person before we tried to roll out to the rest of the company what was going to be an extreme makeover. Initially, I found a little foot-dragging, even among those who I thought I knew well. But we soon had everyone on board and focused on getting exceptional results in a workplace we grew to love."

> I wanted to know I had the commitment from each person before we tried to roll out to the rest of the company what was going to be an extreme makeover.

"We learned how to deal with employee behaviors that needed to change and most importantly, how to deal with folks who have an 'attitude' and because of that suck their coworkers dry of energy. Wow. When it was over, my team was so fired up, I thought they would have helium in their balloons for a decade to come. We could all really see what was possible for each of us and for the company, and we loved it. More important, the team had let go of resentments and "crud" that had built up over the years from letting each other down, even if they were little letdowns. But it all builds up, you know. I hadn't realized how weighed down we all were with some pretty negative emotions and a mistrust of each other. I don't think we were unlike most every other management team…but to be set free from that, WOW, what a difference."

Kathy had a little zucchini and carrot with her next bite of steak and saw that Roger had actually stopped eating, his knife and fork resting in each hand beside his plate. She went on, "The kick-off itself had to embrace a really big idea, one that the whole company could pivot on and change. It was audacious, if I do say so. It was an unreasonable premise. We could tell during the presentation that not everyone bought in. We watched for body language and murmuring. You already heard from Kevin that we'd spotted him as a Doubting Thomas."

Roger nodded for her to go on. "After the kick-off meeting, we went through a series of follow-up moves all designed to help shift the company's culture in the direction we wanted it to go. We had 'the' conversation with anyone we thought might be on the fence about committing to a change of this magnitude. That's where we said, 'I'm so excited about where this team is going. I could be wrong, but my sense is that you don't share the excitement, and that's okay. If this isn't your thing, you have to go find your thing.' Some people jumped that hoop only to get found out by a mystery shopper."

"You mentioned that once before," Roger said. "What's a mystery shopper?"

"That's where everyone gets tested to see how they measure up. Phone shoppers test people's resolve and degree of commitment. We celebrate those who get a 10 and counsel those who could improve. But we keep it as positive as we can. We do that with Hoopla Teams."

"Something sounds like a lot of hoopla."

"Roger, how serious is your situation?"

"Sorry." His grin faded and he leaned forward.

"A Hoopla Team is made up of a cross-section of company members. If it was all management types, it would get too strategic. The Hoopla Team is responsible for constantly rolling out new ideas every couple of months. They oversee the ongoing evolution of the culture, report to the leadership team, and help everyone celebrate successes."

"And from there it's just merrily downhill to a more motivated workplace?"

"Oh, please get real, Roger. I wish it were that easy. But you're from the same real business world I am, so you know there are going to be setbacks, bottlenecks, fumbles—I call these 'Oh, crap' moments, and I know you've had your share of these yourself. If it were all easy and just a flip-of-the-switch thing, anyone willing to energize a workplace with this approach would lose their competitive edge. We know there are going to be wrinkles, and we anticipate those we can and iron out the others that come along. We send off our people to outside seminars and workshops, too."

"Yeah, Kevin told me he'd been to boot camp. Didn't seem as upset about that as I would have been."

"That's just one way to keep everyone enthused. About half of our people have been to one, and they mingle with people from other industries and come back more enthused about the changing culture than ever."

Key Messages for a More Motivated Workplace

Here are some of the core messages for change I share, which you will explore in the pages that follow:

- Commit with all your heart. If you are anything other than a 10 on a 1–10 scale, you are hurting your fellow team members, your customers, and yourself.

- Be unreasonable with yourself. Be unstoppable going after what you want.

- Don't let the little things take you out.

- Call it tight on dysfunctional behaviors—yours and others.' How you do anything is how you do everything.

- Show you care—colleagues, customers, and vendors. In every encounter, make it obvious.

- Celebrate every win. It reprograms the brain for more winning.

- Clean up your messes. If you "blow it," and you will, restore your integrity.

- Use powerful and positive language about what you will do and the attitude you expect from others.

- No more adult daycare! Dysfunctional behaviors must go, whether yours' or of those around you.

- How you do anything is how you do everything. Live with passion and creativity by reprogramming your limiting beliefs.

- You can be as miserable or as joyful as you choose. Those who show they care, who appreciate and celebrate, are leaders of their way of being. They keep a culture focused and people thriving.

- Stop being busy and start doing what matters. Be accountable for results.
- The fastest way to success and happiness is by giving. Life gives to the givers and takes from the takers; the world has a perfect accounting system.

"So it all starts in one day, but there's a lot more to it than that."

"Sure is. But don't take my word and the management perspective on this. Why don't you ask Sara Grimes herself? She was just recognized again at a quarterly company celebration meeting and got to come along on this trip. Let me warn you, though, a hearty steak like this won't buy her story. But a nicely turned wild salmon meal might."

"I'll do just that," Roger said. "Tell me where I can reach her, and I'll pick her brain, too. But I'm already inclined to think you're onto something that could be a big boost for me."

Try this:

- Imagine your workplace as one you are eager to come to.

- Imagine that the only way your workplace will turn around is if you, and only you, are 100 percent accountable for the turnaround. If that were the case, what would you do differently starting tomorrow?

- Identify the ways in which you are part of the problem instead of the solution—whining about what's wrong instead of going to the right people with suggestions, shooting down ideas but not proposing ideas for further progress. Be honest. Really honest. Look at your own behaviors with a magnifying glass.

- Look around and see the fellow employees who are going to need special help to embrace the vision. Use a mirror if you have to.

- Think about it. Do you really believe? Can you commit to this? Can you make it happen and keep happening?

- Do you want this enough to help ensure it can happen? What can you do from all levels of your job?

chapter six

Tales from the Trenches: Front-Line Workers Who Can Think Big

"Think little goals and expect little achievements. Think big goals and win big success."

—David Joseph Schwartz

Sara Grimes was a petite woman with mousy brown hair, and at first glance she hardly looked like the sort of person who might set a company on the path of a cultural change of the magnitude Kathy Pillshard had described. But when Roger Milford met her in the lobby of her hotel, her eyes sparkled with such an inner light that he knew once again he'd been deceived by appearances and that there was much more to her than a quick glance could discern.

At the restaurant, when she opted for baked scrod instead of salmon, Roger said, "Look, get lobster, if you like. I'll buy a dozen lobsters if it puts me on the right path."

"Oh, it's the right path, all right." Her eyes twinkled. "But you're going to have to help yourself as much as anyone about getting on it. In our case, I hardly knew what a tempest of change I was going to stir up when I made my humble suggestion. I just knew that some people looked forward to going to work, and I wanted to be one of them for a change. I also knew the business was kind of just treading water, and it seemed to me that creating a great work environment could be a foundation of a great growth strategy."

> I just knew that some people looked forward to going to work, and I wanted to be one of them for a change.

Roger nodded. "Kathy gave me a brief overview of how the process works. I wondered what it was like from your perspective."

"The first thing I noticed, once the culture change ball was rolling, was that in almost every email and announcement, we were all hearing about the company's vision and its values. I didn't know we had a vision until then, and no one had ever discussed our values. Most of us were just about showing up for the paycheck. That was part of it, and we all started to think about open communication more and getting better at it. We had a lot of transparency—I'm sure if most people know what that means, it's about being more open, honest, and direct. There's nothing really to hide in most companies, and this new transparency made all of us feel more a part of our own destinies and the company's success than ever before. Before you knew it, we really were looking forward to coming to work. I started to hear a lot of stories about people who were having better home lives, too. Beatrice Phillips told me her neighbors wanted to know what had come over her family. They all seemed to be doing better and enjoying life more. It's infectious, viral—in a good way."

Roger nodded. "The only thing I'm thinking now is why it took me so long to reach out and find out more about this. I know it's no cakewalk, but I think my company can do this, too."

"You should have yours eyes open about one thing."

"What's that?"

"This is no overnight thing or a quick fix. It's a complete and ongoing overhaul of your company's culture. In my case, I was a member of a Hoopla Team. That's like a group of in-house cheerleaders to keep things going with a focus on results. It's supposed to be a cross-section of employee types. We had one person from upper management, one from accounting, one from corporate sales, another from marketing, me from the front line, and a few others who gave us a thorough mix of positions and genders."

"Guys cheerlead, too?"

"Yes, and once they get going, they're some of the best and loudest. You see, a culture change is kind

> This is no overnight thing or a quick fix. It's a complete and ongoing overhaul of your company's culture.

of like keeping a campfire going. Left on its own, it will die down. So someone has to keep adding twigs and wood, while others have to fan the flames to ensure it stays bright."

"Does the fire ever threaten to go out?"

"Oh, all the time. We run into bottlenecks, setbacks, and outright fumbles."

"Kathy called those 'Oh, crap' moments."

"Sounds like her. But she's been one of the big drivers of the change—evolution, I like to call it—and it shows in her memos and encouragements. You see, one of the things that has to happen is everyone has to communicate more and be as candid and constructive as they can. We all slip now and again, and we need each other to catch someone who threatens to slip back to old ways, be a bad apple, or even get toxic. The way new people are hired becomes a vital part of it, as well as constant improvement by as many people as possible. Another part of it is getting ongoing encouragement and education from in-house events, as well as outside workshops, seminars, and even those boot camps I thought sounded awful until I went to one. We all do whatever will help us stay focused on the fact that we've all made a choice and we're now accountable for our actions."

"It sounds like an immense amount of effort and energy is being spent on this. How do you all still manage to keep the business going?"

"That's the best part, you see. Doing this makes us better than ever at getting things done, being more interested in our customers and each other. Once we committed, it seemed like our lives got suddenly better. It's like we're family now. I think you've heard how we're doing."

"Yes, I have. Seems like at some point, you made an immense leap of faith, and instead of it all being just another management fad, this approach has taken hold and is working."

Sara poked at a piece of her scrod. She held it up, and a bit fell onto half a crusty roll on her plate. "I'm kind of proud to be the pea that set the big rock into motion, though if Kathy hadn't been open to taking my suggestion seriously and seeking out a way to make it happen, it wouldn't have. But, you see, if you are going to rock your world, you are at some point going to have to shout, 'Bring it on!' and embrace an extra-large size unreasonable promise."

> If you are going to rock your world, you are at some point going to have to shout, 'Bring it on!' and embrace a size extra-large unreasonable promise.

Roger caught something in her voice he had rarely heard from his employees. There was passion there, the kind he had only occasionally heard in job interviews, and then that fire had eventually gone out in even his best hires. Maybe he was going to have to get unreasonable, too.

A Company Becomes "Unreasonable" and Has a Breakthrough

Take the case of one southern financial services system. For many years, it was in the bottom quartile of performance compared to its competitors. It tried many things but could not break through.

The company was doing all the right analyses and starting to understand the nature of its business better, yet it was not using more effective approaches to execute its strategy, attain accountability, and get solid results.

The company had all the excuses in the world. "The first quarter is always a downer," the owner said. "We can count on it every year. It's been that way since when we opened the doors 70 years ago." And he was right. The sales every first quarter were half of what they were the other three quarters.

Then the owner had an idea. "Let's just say we're not going to do that this year and let's choose to make growth happen in the first quarter. In fact, let's grow more than we have in any quarter!"

The company closed out the quarter with more sales than it had in any previous quarter EVER, and it did it with far more profit margin because everyone at the company decided to do that as well. To give the company even more excuses for having a bad quarter, a recession hit, and the company had every reason in the world to not perform.

The challenge that had seemed "unreasonable" had become reasonable.

Unless you push yourself beyond the bounds or everyday comfort, you will likely be stuck in the same groove you are in. You need to commit to results, see them as real, and make yourself accountable to them.

Flipping Unstoppable—Accountability (Here's That Word Again!)

Pat committed to his team that he would bring in 20 new customers by the end of the month. Every person on his team had a commitment to the team, and he was no exception. Of course, for him to get his results, several things had to happen. Marketing had to get the mailings out to the targeted new customers. The people answering the phones had to welcome the customers with such caring enthusiasm that they *wanted* their call transferred to the sales department!

Then the problems happened. Marketing didn't get out their information. "We'll do two next month when we don't have an open house to run." They said this on the 20th of the month when it was obvious they missed their 5th of the month mailing deadline.

The receptionist position turned over when Jessica, who always knew how to get an interested prospect back to the sales department to be converted, left the company. Jim, who now answered the phone, was polite enough but had no idea that the point of answering the phone was to create relationships with people and enroll their hearts into understanding this was the right place and, yes, they need to talk to sales to become a new customer.

Between both of the breakdowns, Pat had only three leads converted by the 25th of the month. It was inconceivable that he would pick up 17 more accounts before the end of the month. He certainly had good excuses on why he could not meet the goal of 20 new customers he'd promised—others had let him down, and it wasn't his fault.

But Pat knew the game. When you're off track, ramp up the focused activity and decide to meet the goal regardless of circumstances.

So Pat picked up the phone 250 times per day for the next four days. He called every client and asked each receptive client who they would recommend as a good fit for what Pat's company did. Clients gave him over 75 referrals that they were willing to call and make introductions. Pat made the additional calls to those referrals, and on the 30th of the month, he had opened 37 new accounts. He was flipping unstoppable.

Results Rock

Don't tell me about the labor pains—show me the baby!

Jodi always explained why something couldn't be done. Excuses come easily. So her boss set the ground rule, "Don't tell me about the labor pains—I don't care how many hours you worked, how many obstacles you hit. Just show me the baby—I want to see the result."

When Jodi learned of this concept, Jodi's results in the marketing department could be sourced to an extra $2 million to the bottom line. Jodi, at first, was as surprised as anyone, but in the end she was a believer.

Try this:

- Consider the most unreasonable goal of the business where you work.

- Identify the excuses that make the goal unreasonable.

- Now, power past them in your mind; picture the path around the obstacles until that goal becomes not only doable, but also reasonable.

- Measure your progress, stay accountable, and get results regardless of all obstacles.

- Set your own unreasonable goals. Don't wait for someone else to request it of you. Those who have great success in life are driven by goals beyond what others expect of them.

- List EVERY possible obstacle to that unreasonable goal. For each one, write beside it at least one strategy about how you will break through and make that happen regardless of the obstacle. Don't leave that sheet of paper until you've done that for every obstacle in advance.

- Take immediate action on one or several of the steps to reach your unreasonable goal. Tell at least two people what you're doing and what your commitment is, and tell them that if you start to have any excuses for why that can't happen, ask them to support you instead of buying into your story. Ask them in advance to not accept ANY excuses and obstacles.

chapter seven

Vision It Possible

"In the absence of a great dream, pettiness prevails."

—Robert Fritz

John F. Kennedy had a vision: "A man on the moon before the end of the decade." And it inspired the seemingly impossible. We had about 15 percent of the needed know-how when he made that declaration.

Bill Gates had a vision that there would be a computer on every desk in America back when most people didn't even know what a computer was!

And that's how it goes for visions. Everyone wins and wins big.

Although a powerful vision is at the core of great culture and performance transformations, visions work at all levels. You don't have to lead an organization to have a vision. Everyone can speak in "vision tongue."

You can have a vision for your company, your department, your family, a project—and you *should* have a vision for *each*! Leaders speak in "vision tongue."

All great visions have three elements, as follows:

- They're short (never more than 10 to 14 words—if you can't fit it on a T-shirt, it's too long), and they use power words like *always*, *every*, or some other way of declaring a result.

- They're visual. You can see a man on the moon. You can *see* a computer on every desk in America.

- They declare your intention to be of service to others. Self-absorbed companies blow up. Ask Enron and WorldCom. Note that Bill Gates never even made computers. His vision was about making the world a better place.

The turning point for a vision is when everyone sees it, gets it, and buys into participating to make it happen. Consider the scene at a bank in Texas, where the bank president was a real dynamo and doing everything he could to share a vision and have everyone get on board, but it wasn't happening as easily as he had hoped. He couldn't get the collective consciousness of all the employees turned around, and he began to be discouraged because most people just kept on spending every day "doing their jobs."

> **The turning point for a vision is when everyone sees it, gets it, and buys into participating to make it happen.**

His goal was to have a more "engaged" workforce, where all employees cared more emotionally about their jobs and, as a result, would be more involved and enthusiastic. His problem amounted to pockets of resistant employees who knew the culture he was suggesting worked quite well in other places, but they felt they had a different situation.

At a group get-together to discuss the change, it became clear that some people were still resisting, fighting the change. All of them were asked to act out what someone who cared less looked like. They did. Then they were asked to show what it looked like to be fully engaged in making sure their team did an extraordinary job in all their assignments. They acted that out.

Then they were put in charge of making sure that if ANY person at their table or any other table looked disengaged, they should call out and ask that person to engage. One group called out about another table saying, "Hey, that whole table over there needs to engage." The whole disengaged table straightened out immediately.

The energy shifted completely the next day. Customers commented all day long about it, and it became the buzz all over town. One of the employees was getting her hair cut and overheard someone saying, "I have hated that bank for years and was planning on pulling out, but something just happened over there a couple of weeks ago, and now it's a great bank. I'm going to stay."

The mood of the entire town changed as all the other businesses talked about the changes at the bank and started to model their behavior after the bank's employees. "Viral" is a hot new word these days, and it doesn't mean passing a cold germ or getting a Trojan horse in your computer. A viral response is when an action meets with a response that takes on a life of its own—for instance, when everyone gets so enthused and energetic that they want to be an active part of improvement for a happier workplace.

The vision is working—people have bought into it. And the power that this vision creates going forward is remarkable! The job of leadership is to build everything and everyone around that vision and talk about it incessantly.

One company grew 35 percent (annualized) the month after their kick-off, inspired by their new vision. That was more than they had grown over the previous 10 years combined! The CEO said, "We talk about our vision at every meeting, in every email, and at every employee interview. We build all of our work plans around our vision. The great thing is, even though it seems like an impossible stretch, I think we all really believe we're going to make it happen. So we will!"

Exploring Your Own Vision

When the consultant finished her talk to Roger Milford and the group of his top managers he had gathered into a leadership team, she sat down, and he got up and said, "Everyone, I don't know where we're going to land with this, but I want us to fix on a vision of how we want to be perceived by our customers, now as well as two years, even five years from now. We need a message that is consistent, strong, and one we can say over and over to ourselves and all our employees, and we'll want them saying it back to us."

"How about 'Show us the money,'" a young man from accounting said.

"That's exactly why we're in trouble," a woman on the other side of the room said. "Every business says that," she explained, "and quite a lot of them sink while shouting it."

The consultant watched Roger, who seemed to have trouble letting go and having his team interact. His hands curled and he leaned forward, a little too eager to speak again. She knew this about him by now. He'd been raised by conscientious, high work-ethic parents in Indiana and had brought those characteristics to his career. He'd also brought a high degree of self-reliance, and sometimes that's an obstacle for executives. A key to this approach is to be open, to listen to everyone better, and to communicate at an honest and respectful level of exchange.

"That's right," Roger said, "We want it to be about our values, how our customers view us. What kind of company do we think we can become? What do we envision? Do we want to make the lives of our customers easier and better, more carefree, more successful? Do we want our own employees motivated instead of scared or angry? Now, let's roll up our sleeves and talk about our vision and be as unreasonable as you like. Okay?"

The consultant caught his eye, and he nodded, grinned sheepishly. He knew he had his hands on the company steering wheel too hard. So he backed off and let others have their say, and it turned out that they realized they were all in the same dilemma and were motivated by the same concerns Roger had.

The woman who had spoken up earlier finally stood and said, "How many of you were glad to come to work today and are glad to be having this meeting?"

A half-dozen hesitant hands went up.

"Come on," she said. "Remember, we're supposed to be brutally honest with ourselves and each other here."

The hands that had gone up went down.

"That's more like it."

Roger glanced toward the consultant, wondering where this was going and if he should step in. The consultant shook her head. Let the woman make her point.

"So, how's this for a vision, then," the woman went on, "picture where we work as a place we love to be. If we do that and let integrity to our purpose shine through to every customer, where would that take us? Wrap your head around that. Can you see it?"

"Impossible," someone muttered.

A surprised smile seeped across Roger's face. The consultant hoped that meant he agreed with the woman's vision and not the mutter from the crowd.

Roger said, "Great. What would happen if we actually accomplished this?"

"Well, customers would talk, and it would be good talk, and they'd bring us all their business and their family's business."

"That would be great. How many of you would love to have that as a vision to inspire us in everything we do?"

Every hand went up.

Roger beamed. "That's it then."

The consultant stood up and said, "It's not impossible. It's improbable and hard but definitely doable. Other companies just like yours have done it. They pictured it, and drove toward it, and kept at it, and it happened. I'm not saying it's easy. But it always starts with a bold and audacious idea. That, my friends, is the whole point of a vision."

ABOUT YOUR COMPANY'S OWN VISION

Vision statements use language to provide a compelling picture of future success. They must reach out beyond the walls of the organization to your customers and anyone with whom your company interacts. They ask that your people commit to something bigger than themselves—this is a trait of all enduringly successful people and organizations.

Let's say you have a chain of skateboard stores or a string of pet stores. You want your vision to project the kind of interactions that will excite your customers to bring their friends around. What are you doing that gets in the way of that? What could you do better? What generates that kind of enthusiasm in your customer base? If it's as simple as all your employees need to demonstrate infectious enthusiasm that your customers catch, then that's your vision!

Some examples as a place to start:

- Every customer comes back and brings a friend.
- Every client is a client for life and brings along their family.

- Every customer calls back asking for a customer service rep by name.
- Every customer is treated like they are the only customer every time.

A vision statement is simply a clear word picture of an end result that is a natural outcome of living your values in service to your customers in an extraordinary way. Nothing less. Nothing more. Resist the temptation to destroy the power of a good vision with corporate speak.

Try this:

- Create a vision for every important project. For example, you could tell your graphic designer that your vision is to have a brochure that pops as bold and cutting edge and inspires action.

- Tell your team members who report to you that you want "Every project to be a work of art that you can write home about."

- Let your kids understand, "Every conversation ends with a smile."

chapter eight

Commit to Your Commitments

"Unless commitment is made, there are only promises and hopes; but no plans."

—Peter F. Drucker

Roger Milford sat near the back of the room full of his top management—his leadership team. He watched the faces and body language of the others, not realizing that his own arms were folded across his chest and that his brow was furrowed.

The consultant brought on board to help with their transition had the floor during the management-only section of the kick-off day and was saying, "In order for an organization to have a huge and profound transformation, EVERY manager must vote in with their full heart. There are reasons people aren't always 'in.' So I'm going to ask you to be extremely honest—to go far beyond lip service as you answer this question: 'On a scale of 1 to 10—with 10 meaning committed out of my mind—how committed are you to a breakthrough?'"

"The typical responses are usually between a 7 to a 10."

"Whenever it isn't a 10, you ask for the reason."

"Some people will say things like, 'I don't have enough time.' Or 'Well, I don't know. Explain breakthrough.' Or 'I'm a practical person. I can't commit until I know EXACTLY what I'm committing to.' For each answer below a 10, you need to help them understand why their answer will end up hurting the rest of the management team because they must be a unified voice for a major breakthrough to happen."

"If the person says, 'I'm a seven because I don't have enough time,' you know that's just an excuse, and you need to defuse all the excuses and stories. The person is saying he or she doesn't have time to do his or her job. This is now part of the job. It's up to you to tell the person to stop using that as an excuse and start choosing to get massive, focused results every day, for the good of this team." At the end of the day, people make excuses because deep inside they think too little of themselves. Working to do whatever job is in front of you really well is the only way out.

"Occasionally, you will come to a tough cookie to crack. Look around now. Pay attention to body language. See anyone?"

Several of them looked Roger's way, but no one raised a hand. He finally figured out the looks and uncrossed his arms. "You mean me?"

"Yes, Roger. You. What would you be? From 1 to 10."

Roger glanced around at the anxious faces of his leadership team, and then said, "Well, I suppose I'd have to be a 10."

The consultant chuckled, as did a few others in the room. "That doesn't sound like a 10 to me. Does it to the rest of you?" They all shook their heads.

> This approach calls for honest conversation and the kind of openness that will allow anyone to communicate with anyone else who is slipping off course—because we all do at times.

"Look, I don't mean to pick on you, single you out, or, worse, bully you. But if you aren't on board and all the way on board, we have trouble here in River City. There can be no faking it with this. This approach calls for honest conversation and the kind of openness that will allow anyone to communicate with anyone else who is slipping off course—

because we all do at times. That's why we need to have team members who take a stand for us when we're slipping. Are you with me?"

Roger nodded, feeling the eyes of all the others on him in a way he'd never experienced before.

"Okay, so we're all getting that's not a 10, and what this team needs is for you to be a 10; otherwise, the team members will see right through you, and they'll think that 'this too will pass' like other initiatives you have started. They can smell out when a management team is giving something lip service versus when every person on the team is committed to the breakthrough."

Roger glanced around, swallowed, and said, "Look, I started this ball rolling. So don't you see, I must be a 10."

Several more in the room chuckled this time. The consultant asked the room, "Okay guys, what do you hear? Is he a 10?"

Every person called it a "No."

"Got it. We need to talk through this. There is a big difference between 'having' to be a 10 and 'committing' to be a 10. 'Having to be a 10' is based on being rational; the problem is as soon as a fact changes, you can slide back to not being a 10 because now you have some 'evidence' that 'this might not work.' When you instead 'commit' to be a 10, that means that you just plain are—it's in your heart. You are committed to a breakthrough, and nothing and no one will get in your way. With that understanding, let me ask you again what your number would be."

"Well, I guess I would be a 10 then." Roger said.

The consultant buckled over in laughter. "Oh, you're goooood. You must have an advanced degree on how to stay on the fence. I know that's not how you run your company on an everyday basis. What do you have to say?"

Roger said, "Okay, well, I guess the only right answer is a 10."

"Good gravy," the consultant says, "We aren't making any progress. How about the rest of you? Is Roger a 10 yet?"

They make a low murmur because, after all, Roger is the boss.

"We can never make this work with that lack of spirit, Roger." She turned to the others in the room and said, "Okay guys, you're the ones who have to work with each other. Now realize, this isn't about Roger. Roger is simply doing what we ALL do sometime or other in our life when we check out on committing to be a part of a team. We've all been there. We'll all go there again. This is when a team needs to take a stand for a human, and the reason you haven't accomplished great results as of yet is that you haven't taken each other on—you wait for someone else to do it and play victim and martyr to those who are in their stuff—complaining behind their back but not dealing with it.

"I'm going to take a seat in the corner of the room and let you talk among yourselves. You have to learn to be frank and help each other move forward. And Roger, they need you to be real and not just give them words but give them meaning."

Roger felt his cheeks flush. But he'd set himself up for this. He'd be a damn fool to walk out of the room at this point. So he braced himself as everyone turned toward him and huddled in closer. His upper management coworkers began to say things like, "Roger, we need you in." The requests went on and on.

After they had all had a chance to coax and encourage Roger, the consultant moved into the huddle and asked, "Roger, when you hear these things, do you think they are sincere in their requests?"

"Yes."

"Do you think they're all wrong?"

"No."

"So, are you willing to make it clear to this team that you're a 10?"

Roger's face felt as flushed as he could ever remember it being.

But he knew they were right, and the feeling swelled in his chest, and he nodded and looked around at each of them. "Thanks, he said. "I'm a 10 and you can count on me." He said it with the conviction and sincerity that confirmed he believed in it.

At that precise point, the chances of Roger turning around his company and creating an improved culture for a more motivated workplace went from barely possible to highly probable for the first time.

Roger's breakthrough was symbolic of what everyone in the company must have if they are all to give to each other as they recommit every day. Months later, the talk was still all around the organization about the amazing transformation of Roger once he threw his heart over the bar.

Try this:

- Ask yourself how committed you are to all you do at work. Be honest, even if it stings.
- How committed do you want those around you to be?
- Think of ways to get into the open everyone's concerns and considerations so you are all pulling with the same enthusiasm and purpose, not some carrying only part of their load, or, worse, others even holding everyone else back.

chapter nine

Have Yourself a Kick-Butt Kick-Off

"The secret of business is to know something that nobody else knows."

—Aristotle Onassis

Roger Milford looked out at the sea of faces and realized this was the first time he had ever seen everyone in the company all in one place. Even at the company picnic, a number of employees often elected to play hooky. He'd let them know that today they all needed to be present. Even Fred Walters from the mail room had made it and wore a surgical mask and sat near the back since they'd gotten him out of a sick bed in order to be present. The faces reflected a range of emotions, from bored resignation to even a touch of nervous fear here and there. He had one or two butterflies himself playing handball in his stomach, even though he'd given a similar kick-off speech to the company's managers earlier in the day.

"Everyone," he said, and the low buzz stopped. "Today marks the beginning of a transformation, and you're all going to be a part of it. It's going to start with me using two four-letter words you don't often hear in the same sentence. Work and love."

He watched the faces, caught a few eye rolls and elbow nudges. He knew the managers would be watching for body language and signs too. "Instead of a place where we dread to come, I want us to look forward to coming to work. Believe it's possible? Well, start to entertain

> **Our vision is nothing less than to make where we work a place we love to be.**

the idea in earnest because that's where we're headed. Our vision is nothing less than to make where we work a place we love to be. You're going to be hearing and seeing that vision a lot. I want you to picture it in your head. It's Monday morning, and you are smiling as you come in the front door."

Almost everyone laughed, and for varied reasons. Much of the laughter had more than a bit of mocking doubt. That was okay. He'd been told to expect that. It was good to have the emotion in the room.

He smiled. "The way we're going to do it differs from a lot of the complex things we've tried. This is really quite simple, by comparison. But we're going to do it thoroughly, and every single one of you is going to be involved. The simple thing is this: We are going to encourage and celebrate every positive thing we do, and we're going to discourage and eliminate every negative aspect of what goes on in the workplace. We will all be measured, and we will be more open and honest about helping each other achieve this transformation. I'm here to tell you that you are going to notice a difference, and your customers are going to notice a difference, and your family and friends are going to take notice. We're going to nurture each other for more positive performances and cure each other of negative practices—simple as that—all day, every day."

MIND READING 101

You're thinking, "You have GOT to be kidding. This wouldn't work at my workplace. I work with master manipulators and saboteurs. They can't be saved. They don't even want to be saved. And alone, I can't do this. Besides, I'm not the boss, so I could never even get my company to do a kick-off, and second, even if we did, there'd be so many fighting it that we would set the record of having the worst results."

Am I a mind reader? No. But I have been around this block for a few decades, and I've heard this conversation several hundred times.

So you're not alone in your thinking. That said, get over it! You can keep playing small, buying into your excuses that you really can't do anything, or you can step up. How would this world even function if there weren't people who were stepping up and making things much better?

It's always an exciting time for me to see the jaws drop at the all-employee kick-off meeting and hear the murmured ripples of disbelief. But as they all make a pact to be more honest with each other and kick off to a new way of doing business, holding each other accountable and helping each other, eliminating excuses and politics, they start to become something they could never have been before—a family.

The laughter had taken on a nervous edge, but that just made Roger smile more. "Keep that picture of a more fun and motivated workplace in your minds. I think you will find us aware of the adjustment pains some of you may experience. You will find us loving and nurturing, but firm. We, each of us, will have standards of expectations about how we will be with each other and customers, we will be measured in respect to the standards, and we are going to develop a zero tolerance of dysfunctional behaviors, including whining, excuses, gossip, and a few others I think you can call to mind. The petty and problematic is out, and the positive is going to be celebrated. Everyone is going to give 100 percent for eight hours every day."

The room had actually gotten quite still. You could have heard a pin tumble sideways across the carpet.

"It's a lot to accomplish in one day, but we are officially started on this path as of today. Each of you has a choice to make, and you'll get the chance to discuss it with your manager. By tomorrow, I will have a Hoopla Team in place made up of a cross-section of representatives from various departments and levels. They'll be responsible for keeping what we start here today going. They'll celebrate and help roll out fresh initiatives to keep our momentum going and to help us work around any setbacks. We're human beings, and, as such, we're going to have a few setbacks, but we want to keep the general momentum going forward and upward."

He gave them a chance to murmur for a second or two while the managers looked around, then went on. "Here are just some of the principles that are going to guide us as we transform." He read from his list:

- Have fun! Work is supposed to be a hoot. Take your work seriously and yourself lightly.
- Be unique. Make your uniqueness matter to the customer.
- No backbiting. Talking behind people's backs creates an unsafe work environment. Conflict should be worked through daily and directly.
- No whining.
- Ask better questions and listen better.
- Systematize everything and keep improving each system.
- State ALL things in the positive. Never say what you don't want. Always say what you do want.
- Be coachable. When people offer an opinion about how you can be better, don't interrupt and tell them why they're wrong. Ask questions and seek to be better.
- Celebrate successes wildly and often.

- Never accept mediocrity.

- Lavish praise at least five times a day. Gratitude and appreciation are the drivers of productivity.

- Always ask yourself, "Am I making the highest and best use of my time?" Identify the bottom 80 percent of your activities and replace them with new activities.

A few heads enthusiastically nodded. The majority of the people looked frozen, as if something way too weird was about to happen, and they didn't want to express an emotion until they knew what the heck was up. Others had their eye-rolling already in high gear and were glancing to co-conspirators, imagining tomorrow's water cooler conversation. "Yeah, right, like they want us to be motivated or something? Then I suppose they'll just give us the shaft some other way."

Roger said, "As we start looking at all the ways we suck the work environment dry, let's first get honest and admit that we *all* do it, and we *all* do it often. If you're listening to this thinking, 'Aha, ol' Roger admits he does this, too,' then you're missing the point. Look only at yourself and ask what you need to change to make sure you are giving energy instead of sucking it dry."

Then the kick-off fun began. That evening, over the next two and a half hours, with all the team members in the room who had helped create the vision helping everyone see and commit, people began jumping out of their chairs with excitement. They knew it may be nearly impossible to make happen, but when they were asked to give their word on would they make it happen, every person in the place shouted "yes." This was hard to believe, since most, when they had walked in, resembled the walking dead and had looked like the only thing they were excited about was retirement, and the sooner that came, the better.

Once they had all agreed to the lofty vision they would make happen, they spent the next hour creating the standards they would live by to make it happen, from how they handled customer inquiries to how they handled mistakes or problems. They all helped set standards about how they would treat each other.

They identified all the "crazy making" behaviors that happen in every workplace, theirs included, that made it resemble adult daycare more than a functional workplace where people could feel safe and be great at what they did.

They discussed not gossiping, not whining, making no excuses, no fault blaming...you name it. They named every behavior that was unproductive, and they created a pact to make those behaviors go away.

> They discussed not gossiping, not whining, making no excuses, no fault blaming...They named every behavior that was unproductive, and they created a pact to make those behaviors go away.

At the end of the two and a half hours, people were so very excited they couldn't contain themselves. Roger said, "Wow, what a night. Do you love our vision?"

"YES!" They screamed in unison with no coaching.

"Are we going to make that happen?"

"YES!" They shouted again.

"Well, this is only the start. Starting tomorrow, when the phone rings, it could be the mystery shopper, and if it is, know you'll be measured on the standards we agreed to tonight. We need to be impeccable. I expect we will all get 10s. What will we get?"

They shouted in unison, "10s."

"And when you do, there will be celebration and prizes. This is just the start. We are going to be a 'top one-percent' company. We are on our way to the vision. Are we going to get there?"

"YES!" They screamed.

"Are we going to make our vision happen?"

"YES!"

"I couldn't be more pleased. We've always been good, and good is the enemy of great. Today marks our beginning on a new path to a level of greatness that you know we're called to be a part of. So, starting tomorrow, let's make it obvious to every customer and every visitor that this is the best place to work if you want to have fun and kick some butt and take some names to make miracles happen. Are you in?"

"YEEEEEES!"

"So am I. See you tomorrow, and let's show the world what we have in us."

The music began with a roar. People were hugging each other. Some were saying things like, "I've been working here for 18 years, and I've hated every day of it, but I can't wait to get to work tomorrow."

Some of the people, who Roger thought would be the biggest troublemakers, who he'd pegged as people who would NEVER get it, got it. Really got it. They were on fire, and they beamed...just plain beamed. Well, who would have thought that?

Try this:

- Stop and picture the vision shared as clearly as you can in your head. Do you see happier people? Can you imagine more motivation?

- Discuss a life and business transforming change like this with your family. If you decided in one day to turn around the way you act around each other every day, could you do it?

- Picture the next day at work after a kick-off event like this. What sort of buzz do you think will be going on?

chapter ten

Hooplas & High Fives & Cheerleading: The Everyday Celebration

"Celebrate. Celebrate. Dance to the music."

—Three Dog Night

The first thing the next morning, Roger Milford fired off an encouraging and celebratory email to the whole staff and walked the halls, listening and fielding questions. He put on his best smile, which he wore in spite of a sharp pain in his back he'd gotten from sitting or sleeping wrong. Still, he went out to share as many congratulations, high fives, and positive encouragements as he could. It didn't take him long to realize he was a little more out of practice at this than he had anticipated, but he soon got back into the swing and realized he used to do a lot more of this sort of thing when his company was smaller. He'd gotten away from the practice.

Outside it was raining, and Roger watched as employees came into the building, shook off their umbrellas, and greeted each other with new enthusiasm. Well, most of them tried to get into the spirit and enthusiasm of the culture change. Although the transformation had launched in one day, it was going to take far longer than that to make the full shift. There were still a number of grinches, grumps, and doubters who would struggle with the idea. Some, he had been told, would not make it. This was no Mary Poppins sort of shift where there was some kind of a wave of a magic wand or sprinkle of magic

> This was no Mary Poppins sort of shift where there was some kind of a wave of a magic wand or sprinkle of magic dust, and everyone was a complete convert.

dust, and everyone was a complete convert. Managers had begun to pair off with any of the employees who had shown or voiced signs of being on the fence. He expected some attrition but would do any replacement hiring with the new culture in mind—all to the good.

Roger's Hoopla Team met and started planning celebrations, initiatives, and training events the first thing the next morning. Through the years, Roger's managerial style had been pretty hands-on. Sometimes he had caught himself micro-managing far more than he should and knew that he did so because those were the times he thought he was the only one who "got it." This new approach meant trusting others more, coaching by way of uplifting feedback, and managing mood as he worked at getting everyone to help each other. It was taking him an effort to hold back his natural tendency to take over. He found this especially important with the Hoopla Team. To his initial astonishment, he found it was more effective to play the role of their coach and cheerleader than their commander-in-chief! He learned that people felt even more successful when he attended the success celebrations and that this led to even more effective action that, in turn, delighted their customers.

WHAT IN THE WORLD IS A HOOPLA TEAM?

Yeah, "Hoopla." I know. You may think that sounds like a lot of happy talk instead of a serious business approach. I don't care what you call it. You can call it the hobnailed boot club.

But you need a team like this to tap the enthusiasm and have it come from fresh standards and initiatives that keep the vision alive and the transformation of your culture happening.

I always suggest a Hoopla Team be made up of 7 to 10 volunteers coming from the enthusiastic employees who are really good at getting stuff done. Each should come from varying positions and departments, with only one executive on the team. If all its members come from management, you'd get lots of strategy, but less engagement by the rest of the organization.

The charge of this team is to sustain and accelerate break-throughs in performance according to an implementation formula. They focus especially on celebrating and documenting successes so that everyone can do more of what works and let go of what doesn't.

The objective is to get the culture change to generate from a grassroots level so that everyone at all levels has more own-ership of the transformation. The team should have as great a cross-section of people as possible so that different depart-ments, genders, and ages are all represented for a diverse and dynamic "movers and shakers" group willing to drive change. The group will rotate new members in and current members out, so many will get the chance to serve.

The charge of a Hoopla Team is to help finalize a company's sales and service standards and get everyone more engaged, consistent, and living the company's vision and values. Meet-ings should be strategic and ask of every initiative and activity

- Is this supporting our vision?
- Is this consistent with our values?
- How are we making this fun?
- How will this be viewed from the customer's perspective?

One morning as he ambled down a major hallway past rows of cubicles on one side and open office doors on the other, a brash young junior executive called out to him, "Have I told you lately, Roger, that you're doing a great job?"

Roger froze and felt his smile ooze off his face to be replaced by a warm flush of blood that lit his cheeks. Then he realized everyone around him was laughing, that the fun was genuine and not mockery. Caught in the moment, he snapped back and laughed, too, hard and freely. This is going to work, he thought. It's really going to work.

Try this:

- Expect good things from the people around you and reward them with palpable appreciation and recognition.
- Realize hoopla isn't silliness or a sign of weakness. It's a demonstration of daily joy.
- Be sincere and don't be afraid to let it show.
- Respect and be kind to each other. You're in this together.
- Don't wait for an annual awards presentation to let people know you value their performances.
- Treat everyone the way you'd like to be treated, and admit it—you're just as happy with a pat on the back as anyone.

chapter eleven

Hooplas & High Fives & Cheerleading: The Ongoing Everyday Celebration

"The more you praise and celebrate your life, the more there is in life to celebrate."

—Oprah Winfrey

Dolores "Dell" Scranton got her first job in publishing in 1976 at a small but prestigious publisher so deep in the heart of the South that the scent of magnolias filled the air and Spanish moss draped the trees that lined the pond next to the main building. But the atmosphere inside was far from anything like a mint julep.

The business was owned by a family, and the two principals were a husband and wife who had migrated south from "somewhere near New York City." With them, they had brought a management style that emulated Simon Legree or any of a number of bosses in the novels by Dickens. They weren't in business to be "nice guys."

A SHIFT IN APPROACH

I want to leave Roger Milford's story for now to stay with the driving principles of the kind of transformation I'm talking about, but with different examples to illustrate that this can happen anywhere.

We'll revisit Roger from time to time to see how he and his company are coming along, but I want to show in varied ways how to get the positives emphasized, and then I'll take some time to show how to work through the inevitable negatives. Keep in mind, too, that a culture change of this magnitude usually affects senior management even more than other employees.

Just FYI, Kathy Pillshard and Sara Grimes both got huge bouquets of roses from Roger's wife, who said, "I don't know what you taught my husband, but I really like the new and improved Roger a lot more!"

This was Dell's first job, and she wanted to be in publishing, but had recently married and felt she needed to stay near her husband's work. He made good money repairing heating and air conditioning, more of the latter than the former. Dell didn't know what normal working conditions on a job were, but she sensed from the first that something was far from fresh in Denmark here. Her husband groused about his job, and she guessed her job wasn't perfect either.

The two owners each had corner offices the size of ballrooms, with Persian rugs and huge teak desks. The workers, like Dell, who proofread, copyedited, and even handled acquisitions, were crammed into tiny cubicles where you could hear an employee asking the person at the next desk to please stop sucking his teeth with such vigor and noise. The employees had a 20-minute lunch break and were docked if they weren't back at their desks when that time was up. They had no lunch or break room, so they had to eat outside or at their desks if it rained, and it rained a good deal of the time. The owners had a dining room to themselves and a resident chef who cooked gourmet meals that the workers could smell as they were being prepared.

At night, one of the owners liked to roam from desk to desk to ensure that no one had more than the one pencil they were allotted, that their desks were tidy, and that the blinds had been pulled to conserve energy. The one time Dell forgot to close her window blind she came in the next morning to find her phone in her wastebasket. A coworker told her that was to tell her that she had her one warning, and if the blind wasn't closed again, it was curtains for Dell.

When Dell got divorced in the mid-'80s, she felt nothing was holding her back from seeking a big-time job in publishing. So she brushed off her resume and landed a job in New York City. She found a small efficiency flat and showed up the first day expecting the worst.

She was knocked off her feet.

The boss's boss, CEO of the company, came through the office on her first day, and he was giving high fives and calling out, "Atta girl, Alice." And, "Great job, Larry." Not only did he know everyone, he was also cheering them on. In all her born days, Dell had never expected or seen anything like it. Even more strange, everyone was shouting back to the head Poohbah as if he were a person like them. And this was in New York City, mind you!

It didn't take long for Dell to realize she was in a far more motivated workplace than she'd been in at her former job. As she described it later, "Why we didn't gather up

> It didn't take long for Dell to realize she was in a far more motivated workplace than she'd been in at her former job.

torches and pitchforks and storm those corner offices and put the owners' heads on spikes is beyond me yet."

Dell rose up in the company, made her way through middle management, and eventually all the way to the top—CEO. She had a corner office herself now, though noted with irony that it was a quarter the size of those owners' offices from her first job.

She found, too, that of the management styles she'd seen, she gravitated herself toward that of mutual respect, cheerleading, high fives, hoopla, and having fun. She learned there was a fine line between being patronizing and boosting the parade, and that when she had to be serious, she could. But life was better, work was a joy, and her numbers were shooting through the roof, which is an especially keen thing when you're housed in a 52-story skyscraper.

She had remarried, and her children had grown, and one fall day she was at the college soccer game of her daughter, Lil. A competing publisher spotted her in the stands and kidded her in a way that was not really kidding as they shook hands. "You're kicking my butt again this year, and try as I might I haven't been able to hire any of your people away. How do you do it?"

Dell smiled to herself. Here he was to cheer on his child, to boost her, yet he apparently didn't realize that approach works at the office, too. Your employees aren't your children, although one or two may act up as if they were at times, but they like daily appreciation, recognition, and encouragement.

> Your employees aren't your children, although one or two may act up as if they were at times, but they like daily appreciation, recognition, and encouragement.

She sat back and watched the game, where her not-so-secret secret of success was being enacted before them as players high-fived, coaches shouted positive encouragement, fans celebrated and cheered, and parents were there all the way to demonstrate their support. The players were playing a game and having fun at it. That's how a motivated workplace can be, too.

Try this:

- Show by example how you want and expect others to behave as they nurture and encourage each other.

- Your Hoopla Team should bring out a new truth or standard every two months to ensure that the momentum you engendered on kick-off day keeps going. The process involves rolling out a succession of new and fresh layers that all support the culture change. Make it fun, not preachy.

- Host quarterly all-employee ceremonies.

- Encourage participation by as many employees as possible in seminars, workshops, and training programs that instill the values of your culture.

- Keep your successes visible. Dedicate wall space to a gallery of success. Continually post success stories.

- Explain expectations and how those expectations will be measured. Members of great sports teams challenge each other through every play. It works here, too.

chapter twelve

Measure Everything!

"Show me how a person is measured and I'll show you how he will behave."

—Various

Bobby Keller had been working as a grocery checkout clerk for the better part of a year, halfway through his senior year of high school and up to the time a number of his former schoolmates were heading off to college. He was joking with a couple of them while sliding bar-coded goods across the scanner as he ignored the customer across from him.

Gladys, the clerk supervisor, came over and slid a "Lane Closed" sign across the end of his lane. "Hey, I didn't know I was due for a break. I'll come out and shoot the breeze with you guys."

"It's not a break. I want a word with you, Bobby." She went back to her usual spot beside the bulletin board to keep an eye on the 15 lanes that were her responsibility.

"Uh, oh. Looks like I've ticked off Missus Hitler," Bobby said to his friends as they headed out the door without him. It was loud enough for Gladys to hear, but he didn't care.

He closed out his drawer, ran his fingers through his long hair, and went over to Gladys, who finished talking to a sacker and turned to him.

"What?" he said.

"I had a customer come up to me and ask if I knew that fruit bruises. I said I was aware of that. He said, 'Well, that boy over there isn't.' He pointed at you, Bobby."

"Look, if I…"

"Don't get defensive. I'm telling this to help you."

"Okay, I guess. Whatever."

"I've a whole list of complaints about you, Bobby. In addition to bruising fruit and denting cans, you've made errors with coupons, talked with others instead of your customers, and even made inappropriate jokes about products people were purchasing, a strict no-no."

For the first time a ripple of fear crept up Bobby's spine and hesitated just below his ears. Oh, crap. He had the car payments, and he'd been saving up to get a small efficiency apartment, away from his parents' house. "Am I going to be fired?"

"I want you to think about things like telling Mrs. Adsner that she was sure buying a lot of ice cream. You can see she has a problem with her weight. The ice cream was for her daughter's birthday party. But you managed to hurt her feelings."

"Look, we just had that big flapping meeting about how everyone was supposed to have more fun at work. I was just kidding around, trying to lighten up. Isn't that what we're supposed to be doing more of?"

"I think you know the difference between a joke and what is personal or hurts someone's feelings."

He tried to stay cool, but a lump was growing in his throat, and he had a bad clammy feeling in his stomach. "Am I being fired? Just tell me that."

"No. I'm giving you a task for the rest of this week. Our sister store across town is going through the same process, and I'd like you to act as a mystery shopper. All you have to do is be a customer at different times and take notes about the clerks. Okay?"

"Cool." Relief ran all the way down to his shoes.

MEASURE WHAT MATTERS

If it matters to creating your results, measure it. Measure everything that matters.

"What's a mystery shopper?" you may ask. You may even be familiar with mystery shoppers in retail sales settings, the ones who seek to catch employees not performing at their best. Well, the concept is similar here, except it works with any business.

I suggest phone mystery shoppers, ones who check the company's reception, too; include the same kind retailers use, but mystery shop how your executives interact and yourself as well. It's one thing to commit to showing you care for everyone more, to being more caring and human. But do you deliver?

First decide what matters. How you answer your phone matters. One goof up could cost you a million dollar deal or more. How you greet people matters. How you ship goods matters. How you recover from mistakes matters. You get the point.

When you mystery shop one area at a time with extremely clear expectations, coaching, and celebration, suddenly people become attentive to what matters. Go figure.

If you're not shopping, you're guessing. People can look busy, but they can be ruining your business, and you have no idea what they're doing to make that happen until it's too late.

As long as you make the shopping fun and celebratory with instantaneous coaching, results will shift, and there won't be a negative reaction to shopping.

When he reported for his shift at the first of the next week, he came 15 minutes early so he could speak with Gladys. He handed over the notes he'd taken.

"What do you think?" she asked.

"Some of those clerks are wonderful. Some are awful."

"In what ways?"

He looked down and then up into her waiting hazel eyes. "Well, mostly the same things people complained about with me."

"Are you willing to commit to improving on those things yourself?"

"Yes. Yes, I am," and he meant it all the way to his toes. What is more, his performance at work garnered a great deal of notice and positive feedback.

Even Mrs. Adsner pulled Gladys aside one day and said, "Whatever did you do to the boy? He sure seems to sparkle and enjoy his job now. Why, it's night and day. Did you send him off to military school boot camp or something?"

"Well, let's just say he found out that having fun isn't just wise cracking, that it can come from the satisfaction of doing a better job. Once people started letting him know, he's been beaming like a broadcast tower with good news every day and even giving pep talks to the other clerks. He made a commitment, and he's more than living up to it, even though that meant working around one or two obstacles, like not letting on to his friends that he's just doing us a favor by showing up. He actually seems eager to come in now."

"Well, if you ask me," Mrs. Adsner said, "it's not the same boy at all, just one who looks exactly like him. This one has a whole different attitude."

Honest Feedback After Measurement

One of the absolute keys to a workplace worth working in is a level of honesty that encourages the truth when someone isn't pulling his or her weight, candor between employees about each other's efforts, and the straight stuff from everyone when it comes to feedback that can make a workplace improve.

> One of the absolute keys to a workplace worth working in is a level of honesty that encourages the truth when someone isn't pulling his or her weight.

When you agree to do something and then get hit with an obstacle, do you assume all bets are off and cash in your chips? Or do you remind yourself that an agreement is an agreement, so you give yourself a moment to figure out how to get back on track? You realize your integrity is on the line.

Life is filled with people who believe obstacles invalidate a deal. "Yes, I know that was my quarterly goal, but the economy…" "Yes, I know I said I'd finish that project, but I forgot that our family reunion was coming up that weekend, and I had to help plan the kids' activities." "Sherri didn't get her part of the report to me, so I wasn't able to finish my part."

Nothing will hold you back from success in life more than giving up when you hit a hurdle. When people who don't "get it" hit a snag, they might say something like, "Things got too complicated, so I decided it just wasn't worth it to keep on trying." Those who create win after win in life respond differently—they throw their hearts over the bar, knowing the rest of the team will follow.

The language of those who win often is different, too. They say, "Well, things have changed, as they always do, so what do I need to do next so I can finish this project?"

If persistence is the key to success, then commitment is the breakfast of champions. When an obstacle comes your way, don't waste time looking for ways to cave—look for all the ways you can clear that hurdle—in style. Why? Because you said you would.

> When an obstacle comes your way, don't waste time looking for ways to cave—look for all the ways you can clear that hurdle—in style.

You are as good as your word. You make or break your reputation based on what you commit to and when (and how) you deliver the goods. Relationships are built on trust, and trust comes when commitments are kept.

Let neither rain, nor snow, nor any other obstacle stop you. If you're tempted to toss in your cards when the odds start stacking up, just remember to commit to the power of your words—no less than 100 percent.

Try this:

- Be a person of your word. When you make a promise, keep it. When you say you'll do something, do it. Use the language of winners by saying, "I'll do it!" instead of "I'll try." Be unreasonably committed to your promises and refuse to give yourself an out when things go south.

- Consider how you meet the objectives of the person you report to and think about the order of what you do. Make lists. Put stars by the hot tasks that will be most critical or need to be done first. Don't quit until you do them. Your self-esteem will flourish, and you'll find that every week you're capable of more as you have stretched your muscles to be more powerful than the obstacles you hit.

- Commit to help others, too. If someone doesn't get you a report on time, politely nag them until you get it. If that doesn't work, camp at their feet until they absolutely can't stand it anymore. Finishing the job will be frosting on the cake compared to the pressure of having to deal with your looming presence.

- Commit to being a creative thinker. When the economy takes a dive—and it *will* from time to time—figure out what other markets you can tap into or what creative approaches you need to take so you can make up for the deficit.

PART III

The "How To" Toolbox for Making Any Workplace Better

chapter thirteen

Get a Brand New Attitude

"The greatest discovery of my generation is that a human being can alter his life simply by altering his attitudes."

—William James

"I can." "I can't." "I'm not good enough." "Good stuff just happens to me." "I always get sick every winter."

Explanatory styles. We all have them—the filters through which we run all of life's events.

Scientists now know that every thought creates a sudden shift in your body. Just reading the preceding ideas emotionally triggered your pancreas and your adrenal glands to get busy secreting hormones. Different areas of your brain surged with increased electrical currents, causing neurochemicals to be released. Your liver, not to be left out, began processing enzymes that were not present the moment before. Your thymus gland and spleen sent out not-to-be-ignored messages to the body to shift your immune system. There's more…but you get the idea. Thoughts change your body.

Your mind has a tremendous capacity to change your body and your life.

Even more fascinating, every person has the ability to reprogram the filters through which he hears things—but first he needs to have a clue that what he is hearing is never exactly what is said.

IF ATTITUDES WERE CONTAGIOUS, WOULD PEOPLE WANT TO CATCH YOURS?

Is today a good day or a bad day? It's neither. It's just another day. You assign the meaning.

So maybe there have been some things that happened today that you interpreted to be "good"—your kid got news of good grades; a client bought a big deal from you.

Or perhaps this is a day where you have a series of things you are interpreting as being "bad"—the bus splashed you at the corner, and you've had wet socks all morning; your spouse had the nerve to pick a fight this morning, and you took the bait.

Well, regardless of circumstances, as you assign meaning, you are also choosing your attitude. You can have all kinds of "crud" hit and still decide to enjoy the fact that you're not six feet underground today.

Whatever happened to you, your coworkers and clients deserve to have you "interpret" the day as good and make your attitude contagious AND worth catching.

And let me tell you, attitude is something customers notice immediately. If you want them to go away with a smile and come back next time with their friends, you need to be constantly vigilant about the attitude everyone is projecting. If most of you have positive attitudes, but the customer is exposed to one bad attitude, it reflects on all of you, on your whole company's culture, and it will impact your business.

Every thought and image and experience that comes to you is instantly filtered. A college professor writes the same note on the top of the paper of three different students, "There is so much more here."

One student thinks, "Oh my goodness. I'm going to flunk this course. He thinks I missed the point entirely! I always seem to miss what's important. I'd better start packing my bags because I'm never going to make it in college. I'll probably end up working at Uncle Pete's factory all of my days...and marrying a mean and ugly wife."

> Every thought and image and experience that comes to you is instantly filtered.

Another thinks, "He'd like me to explore other parts of this. I'm going to see him after class on Wednesday and tell him I'd like to write another paper on those areas. Maybe he's thinking he wants to make sure I get an A in the course by going deeper."

Yet another reads into it, "I have really challenged my professor's thinking with my paper. I can see how I opened his eyes to there being so much more that he hadn't even thought of before."

The list of interpretations in endless!

It is through those filters, though, that great things or complete disasters can and do happen.

It plays out in the workplace.

YOUR ATTITUDE
By Charles Swindoll

The longer I live, the more I realize the impact of attitude on life.

Attitude, to me, is more important than facts. It is more important than the past, than education, than money, than circumstances, than failures, than successes, than what other people think or say or do. It is more important than appearance, giftedness, or skill. It will make or break a company...a church...a home.

> The remarkable thing is we have a choice every day regarding the attitude we will embrace for that day. We cannot change our past...we cannot change the fact that people will act in a certain way. We cannot change the inevitable. The only thing we can do is play on the one string we have, and that is our attitude...I am convinced that life is 10 percent what happens to me and 90 percent how I react to it.
>
> And so it is with you...We are in charge of our attitudes.

A supervisor challenges one of his employees to be more thorough on a project. The employee's brain, based upon his explanatory style, can come up with a whole range of possible interpretations: "He never likes what I do. Isn't it ever good enough?" "He's just picky. I'll ignore this, and he'll just let it slide." "He really wants me to win on this project. I sure appreciate his insights. I'm going to ask him more questions. I think he sees that I'm management material."

What's so fascinating about filters is that each individual tends to have a certain "filter twist" through which they run all things—and it's completely different from every other person's "filter twist." That twist is largely dependent on how they feel about themselves based on the key messages they have received about how lovable or unlovable they are.

Here's what we know about filters. If an individual grew up with a parent, a teacher, a nun, whoever, telling them they weren't okay, then when you give them input on something, they will most likely hear it as an attack and blame you for being the person who is wrong in making the request. "How could you be so insensitive!" is what goes on in her mind.

So let's get honest here. If your parents were June and Ward and your brother was Wally, and nobody in your family gave you hurtful messages, then it was one of your teachers or some other human who got to you with a "you're-not-okay" message. NOBODY escapes this little life mess. That's why teenagers exist—to mess and be messed with.

People who don't feel good about themselves make a point of putting down others—so, if you've lived for more than a week, somebody's already gotten to you. There are plenty of people in their own private "not-okay" chair who want to put you there instead.

But YOU, and only you, can choose your explanatory style. Without an interruption to a naturally negative explanatory style, you

> YOU, and only you, can choose your explanatory style.

may interpret someone telling you the sky is blue as, "Hey, now you expect me to change the color of the sky! What up?" or "That must mean it's going to be a bad day because I always have bad days when the sky is blue."

The good news—bad explanatory styles can be changed.

Martin Seligman, author of *Learned Optimism*, has done profound research that shows that optimists—those with a positive explanatory style—tend to be far more successful than those who interpret events as negative and permanent.

His research shows that successful people explain good things as positive and permanent, "That's how it always is for me."

They discuss less-optimal results as not likely to happen again, "That's just not like me."

Most conflict in the workplace, in marriages, and in any relationship is a result of someone's filter (messed up from a damaged youth—and who didn't have a fair amount of damage?) that hears the worst possible interpretation and then fights against the other person as if they actually said it—even when they didn't say it and, moreover, don't mean it!

What's shocking is that the person with the damaged and negative filter can fight for hours, days, and months for his point that the other person is wrong—despite the fact that the other person never said or thought the thing in question! You've been there?

So *that's* why we only see world peace on T-shirts!

The great thing about filters is that once you know you have one, you can change it for a powerful shift in results. There is no longer the need to hear the worst, imagine the worst, and, therefore, fulfill the promise of making the worst come to be.

Try this:

- As an experiment, for every substantial conversation you have, write down the exact words the person said. Go back to the person and ask, what I think you said was, "Blah, blah, blah." Is that correct?

- Then tell that person what you interpret that they meant. Ask them if you interpreted correctly or if there was anything that you put into it that wasn't there. When they make adjustments, again repeat those and ask if you heard correctly.

- Make a log of the findings of misinterpretations. You will undoubtedly find a pattern. For example:

  - You assumed they didn't like you. In fact, they were not even thinking about you, and it isn't personal. As the saying goes, "Most of the time you're only an extra in somebody else's soap opera."

  - You assumed they were saying you were doing something wrong when you weren't. Once again. Maybe "they" hadn't noticed you were actually doing anything.

  - You assumed that they were trying to say something to hurt you. Well…by now you get the idea.

- Set the intention that whenever you hear a request or a thought from another person, you will run it through the best possible filter, the one that says she is on your side and wants the best for you. (Decide to implement reverse paranoia.)

- Breathe. Life just became infinitely better. You're going to have more success in life and in relationships. Why? Because your filter said so.

chapter fourteen

Enthusiasm:
Light That Fire in Your Belly

"Depression is often just anger without enthusiasm."

—Steven Wright

Fred Perkins used to love his retail job at a sporting goods store. It fit with his interests, was colorful, and he met a lot of really cool people at work. Lately, though, he found himself dragging his feet on the way to work, even after a couple double latte grandes. Why? What was once fun had become the same old, same old and, worse, he'd let it. So he started to ask himself why he'd taken this job in the first place. Aside from watching sports on television, he used to participate a lot more. He was a jogger, an avid archer, and had been toying with taking up golf for a couple of years.

When It Fades to Black

Let's face it, enthusiasm is a real hard thing to fake. I hear you on that.

Enthusiasm is not something that is granted to some and denied to others. Have you ever met a two-year-old who wasn't enthusiastic? We come prepackaged with enthusiasm. A two-year-old is so fascinated with the wrappings of birthday gifts—he or she can play with them for hours!

So then—what happens to us?

Some of us choose to be in touch with our inner enthusiasm, while others allow it to go dormant or even to mask it.

But it's as essential to life as food and water. Enthusiasm is the essence of all success. Without it, nothing great happens. It is a moment-by-moment choice.

So Fred got curious. He started looking at product lines, turning the colorful pages of catalogs and trade magazines, teasing himself into wondering what was coming next. Some mornings, he got up early and ran for a buzz unlike that from caffeine. He went out on the archery range again and felt the wind tug his hair, allowed for trajectory, released arrow after arrow until he was hitting mostly the center bull's-eye again. He even bought a trial set of clubs. He got moving, got active again. He found himself talking to others with more animation at work, and people started coming to him in the store because he seemed really to care. Explaining his interests to others made him bubble again, and that sort of enthusiasm didn't escape the notice of his customers or the boss.

Moreover, Fred remembered he used to have a goal. One day he wanted to open his own store in a small town, and thinking about the next steps it would take for that gave him even more energy. He started keeping a composition notebook of how his store might look someday, even sketched a few floor plans. He was having fun at work again, and it showed. His sales were up, he got along with his coworkers better than ever, and he found himself looking forward to coming to work again.

We've all had times in our lives when we lost our enthusiasm. What keeps us there is blaming others for putting us there. In fact, *nobody* can put you there without your consent.

> We've all had times in our lives when we lost our enthusiasm. What keeps us there is blaming others for putting us there.

So if you're there, how do you break out?

Demonstrate your enthusiasm for life. Let it radiate in everything you do until you infect everyone around you. If you live your life that way, you will have lived the life of a hero.

Try this:

- Remember that results flow from determination and enthusiasm. You always have a choice.

- Change your accepted beliefs about yourself. If you've always felt that you were a deadpan personality, decide to believe differently. If you think you're not exciting, stretch yourself today to blow away your family and coworkers with your vivaciousness for something. *Anything.* Just *decide* to come alive. It IS a decision.

- Set yourself up for every experience as if it's the first time you've done it. Have you ever lived vicariously through a four-year-old at the beach? It's all just so *amazing* in their eyes. And it should be in ours.

- If pretending it's your first time doesn't do it, pretend it's your last. Watch a sunset and *know* it could be your last. Have a conversation with a coworker as if it's your last time to connect with a person on Earth, and you want to make it count. Dig into a project as if it will be your legacy.

- Make the choice to participate fully. For everything you do today, whether it is a conversation with a coworker, a friend, or a child, or doing a task, decide to "show up fully" and pour all of yourself into it. Listen like you've never listened before. Decide to care like you've never cared before.

chapter fifteen

Life Balance: Show Up Fully No Matter Where You Are

"Be aware of wonder. Live a balanced life—learn some and think some and draw and paint and sing and dance and play and work every day some."

—Robert Fulghum

Tim Moore was on the way to the airport, weaving through what was at least Saturday traffic, but his mind wasn't on the road or the faded brown Volvo that had just cut him off, driven by a guy who was now shaking a fist out his window as if Tim had been at fault.

What bugged Tim was that his son Zack played in a district final football game today, and Tim was going to be twelve hundred miles away, in a meeting. He'd also had to break a promise to his daughter Mackenzie about helping her draft and revise her essay for a school contest.

Suddenly, it hit him. He didn't want to be in any stupid meeting. He was resenting it already, and he probably wasn't going to be at his best. He reached for his cell phone, eased to a left lane to let a truck surge from a ramp into the lane where he'd been, and he thumbed down until he got to Bob's number.

"Yeah, what is it?" Bob answered.

"This meeting we're having to sit face to face and discuss the terms of our agreement, is that a breaking point for you?"

"What do you mean?"

"I mean, if we have it next Wednesday instead, would that work? I'd really like to spend the weekend with my kids."

"Oh, sure. Fine. I hear you. It's our anniversary here, and to tell you the truth, I was in a little hot water myself. Not that Sylvie's hard to be with. Actually, there's a little crab cake restaurant up the coast, a shack really, but one we've both been promising ourselves we'd get back to. Wednesday is fine."

Tim clicked off the phone and started to ease his way back to the right and look for the next exit ramp. He smiled to himself. He felt good and alive for the first time today. That urged in a rush up inside him, and he reached to turn on the radio.

What just happened?

Tim realized that if he could show up 100 percent for work, he could do the same for when he was home with his family. Some people get it the other way around and need to remind themselves that if they're 100 percent at home, they should give the same heartiness at work. Regardless of how you rate yourself on the balance scale of life, sometimes you have to reel back, adjust, and reassess your priorities.

> Regardless of how you rate yourself on the balance scale of life, sometimes you have to reel back, adjust, and reassess your priorities.

You've heard people talk about having "balance" in their lives. They portray it as a teeter-totter. You either have family or you have a job—either you're up or you're down. Which one will you choose?

Hogwash.

You can have career and family, and you can do both well. The point is to fully show up wherever you are. That's the part most people miss.

Two Sides to a One-Dimensional Picture

A lot of people who are serious about how they do business think they need to be two kinds of people. I don't buy that, and I don't want you to either, unless you crave being diagnosed as a schizophrenic.

The thing with achieving any kind of balance is awareness. Are your priorities straight? Do you work well and thoroughly when at work? Do you give your family the kind of value and respect they deserve of your time? Or does one spill over into the other?

By emphasizing positives at work and interacting with your coworkers to achieve that, you may be surprised to find that you start doing the same at home, in that seemingly quite different context, to the eventual delight of your spouse and children.

Your family has a culture too, and when you start communicating openly and honestly in an effort to improve the way you get along, you'll be surprised, and so will your family. Just try it. Go home tonight and ask open-ended questions and listen without interrupting. Really. Just try it. Your teenagers will no doubt say something like, "Hey, what's going on here? You're listening."

And while you're at work, being present there means you aren't just doing what is asked of you; you are wide awake, looking for opportunities to add value, and you are jumping at every chance. You're having fun being amazing at what you're doing.

There's an old line that states, "Wherever you go, there you are." Whether you interpret this as corny or Zen mystic wise, the point is that wherever you are, you will be better off if you show up fully.

Ellen Galinsky, author of *Ask the Children*, asked children the question, "If you were granted one wish to change the way your mother's or father's work affects your life, what would that wish be?"

Fifty percent of parents predicted that the child's top choice would be to have more time together. In fact, only 10 percent of kids said they would like more time with their mothers. Only 15 percent said the same about their fathers. Contrast this with the 34 percent of kids who said what they want most is for their parents to be less stressed. Only two percent of parents guessed that this would be their child's highest priority.

It's not more of our time that our kids want but rather our vivaciousness—to be fully alive and enthusiastic wherever we are at any moment.

So do you fully show up wherever you are? Or are you quasi-committed? Sometimes we have good intentions but just never get there.

Are you the kind of parent who talks about balance and blames your employer for pulling you away from your kids, yet has the television on while you're with them, polluting their minds with negative messages? When was the last time you had a heart-to-heart conversation with each kid individually to find out what is important to them and what they'd like from you to improve the relationship? It's hard to do that with the television on.

When you leave home to go to work, do you say, "Daddy *has* to go to work now" or do you say, "Daddy *gets* to go to work now?" A tiny difference, perhaps, but one that signals whether or not you intend to be fully present where you're going. Be careful. Little minds are learning patterns for their own lives.

Balance means fully living wherever you are—being fully present to your friends when with your friends, with your kids when with your kids, with your spouse when with your spouse, and at work when you're at work. If you're thinking about your bowling league during the budget meeting, your numbers

> **Balance means fully living wherever you are.**

might be off. If you're trying to figure out your fantasy league draft picks while you're playing catch with your son, you might take one on the kisser. And that would be called justice.

Some of the best parents work 50 hours a week or more and are amazingly connected with their children in extremely functional ways. Some of the worst parents are stay-at-home mothers or fathers who watch television all day—know every soap opera, sleep through most of the day, and yell when their kids interrupt their otherwise unproductive lives by asking a question. Sounds rough, but we all have friends who fit these descriptions. In fact, there's a little bit of this in all of us. It's just a matter of degree.

Resolve today to make a commitment to be where you're at. When you're at work, be productive in knowing exactly what the company objectives are. Hanging out at the water cooler and surfing the Internet don't signify a mind and spirit fully present and engaged.

Most of the highest performers know how to get their work accomplished and get out the door to be present with their friends and family. They are extraordinarily skilled at choosing the highest objectives and finding effective systems and processes to get those objectives accomplished with ease.

Strugglers, on the other hand, often waste a tremendous amount of time each day and get distracted easily. They work an enormous number of extra hours to cover up the fact that they're not getting results.

Balance is about fully showing up wherever you are and deciding to enjoy being there. And that, like everything else in life, is simply a decision.

SO, WHAT'S UP WITH ROGER?

"Kathy?"

"Yes. What is it, Roger?"

"Your voice is faint. Are you on a cell phone?"

"Yep. We're on a bus, 50 of us, headed for a pizza lunch. It's a celebration for a department that did well."

"If you don't mind, I have a quick question for you."

"It's down the hall, to your left, Roger, same as it's always been."

"I don't mean the men's room. I want to know if you ever had a relapse."

"Sure. A couple or three times."

"What did you do about it?"

"I sent myself to a boot camp. Had a great times too. Came back to the office ready to wrestle grizzlies."

"Each time?"

"The process is all about maintenance and moving forward once it's started, rolling out new initiatives, staying fresh and on your toes. It's for everyone, and management usually has a harder time than anyone. Why?"

"My Hoopla Team thinks I should go to one of those camps. I had one grumpy day, and a mystery shopper caught me."

"Well, good for them. They're just helping you, Roger, nurturing you. Do what they say. It'll be good for you. You'll have more fun than you expect, and I'll bet next time you think twice before you're grumpy at work."

Try this:

- Decide that wherever you are at the moment, you have enough time to be fully with the people you are with.
- Never say, "I don't have enough time" again. Replace it with, "I'm choosing to prioritize here."

chapter sixteen

Values as Your True North

"Values provide perspective in the best of times and the worst."

—Charles Garfield

Tim Forbes, a software programmer in San Jose, has had several jobs over the last few years. Truth be told, he hadn't really been happy since his college days at Cal Poly, Pomona, and that was more the result of beer parties and a semi-steady girlfriend back then. He told his neighbor that he wasn't happy in his newest job and wanted to find a new one. The neighbor asked him, "Are you moving toward a new job, or are you moving away from a mess?"

"Well, if I'm honest with myself," he said, "I suppose I'm running away."

"That's unfortunate," the neighbor said, "because there was obviously some lesson you missed while there, mistakes that you'll probably repeat. I suggest you stay and learn the lesson so that you can move toward something—otherwise, we'll be having this exact same conversation in another year when you're looking for your next job."

Tim left, though, and started a new job, which he recently lost. Same story...different day.

The trick here is to be honest with yourself. If you're getting married, it's easy to say you're moving toward a relationship—but you might be moving away from being alone. That's a very different reason to get married, and not a very good one. How many divorced and/or miserable people are out there raising their hands on this one?

You will find that almost every bad decision followed from a violation of a value—a moving away from a fear instead of moving toward something you love.

> You will find that almost every bad decision followed from a violation of a value—a moving away from a fear instead of moving toward something you love.

You've made some good decisions, and you've made a few lousy ones. Welcome to the human race. If you've been around long enough, you may have even bought Beta tapes, bell-bottom pants, mood rings, pet rocks, and platform shoes, too.

But what can you learn from history to improve the odds of making better choices? Let's do an autopsy on the decisions you've made that have killed deals, killed relationships, reduced your success, and otherwise created general chaos in your life.

For example, you needed to meet a goal or quota, so you did the wrong thing by the client. You thought the client and your boss wouldn't notice. That didn't work. You violated your value of always doing the right thing by the customer, and a bad result was your reward.

You had to get home early to meet with friends, so you didn't double-check that project before sending it out to the client. You lost the deal because you didn't uphold your value of quality work. Again, bummer result.

You were in a pinch to fill a position so you hired someone you *knew* just didn't share your values. Twenty-four hours after the start time, you know you have a problem.

In each of these cases, you made a decision that deep in your gut felt wrong before you even made it. That butterflies-swirling-like-a-flush-down-the-porcelain-bowl feeling is all that's needed to know for certain that we blew it. Gut feelings are not like weathermen. Gut feelings are never wrong.

Let's make this easy. Psychologists tell us that all emotions are rooted either in love or in fear. Anger, for example, is a symptom of fear. You can't be angry if you're not afraid. Joy is based in love. You can't feel bliss without having love at the core.

Fear is a "moving-away-from" emotion. Love is "moving-toward."

Analyze the disastrous decisions you've made, and a pattern of "moving away" from something will generally emerge. Moving away from missing a quota. Moving away from confronting a problem. Moving away from one company or boss as opposed to moving toward a bigger calling—thus, the saying, "Out of the frying pan, into the fire."

So the next time you need to make a decision, ask yourself if you're moving away from something or moving toward something.

The amazing part about the "moving away from" syndrome is that people repeat the same patterns. Julie keeps leaving controlling bosses. Joe keeps divorcing the same wife with different names—each of whom is "cold-hearted." Hmmm, makes you wonder if the problem is really "out there."

If you really watch people in your life, you will notice that they keep leaving jobs for the same reason they left the previous job; people who can't get along with people at one workplace can change workplaces, and then they manage to

> The next time you need to make a decision, ask yourself if you're moving away from something or moving toward something.

find a company with a lot of "jerks" like the place they just left. If you can observe this pattern in others, might it ever, possibly, with even a remote chance, be a pattern that you may have?

Before making any decisions, ask yourself if you are moving toward or away from something.

Try this:

Before making any major decision, ask these two questions:

- Is this in alignment with my core values?
- Would this decision be made out of love or fear? Am I moving toward something, or am I running away?

The discipline of always asking these two questions, and answering them honestly, really will improve the quality of your life.

chapter seventeen

Bravely Go Beyond the Job Description

"Some of us will do our jobs well and some will not, but we will be judged by only one thing. The result."

—Vince Lombardi

Albert Johnson had just moved to a small town, too far out to be a suburb, but close enough that he could make a long commute to get to his office in Omaha. He lived in a small cottage by a lake. The waterfront property, an acre and a half, cost far less than a three-bedroom ranch home closer to his office. If the gas prices didn't eat him alive on the commute, he was going to have a lower cost of living and live in a constant vacation setting. Cool.

So he went out to his car in the morning, and "click"—nothing. He turned the key again. Same thing. Uh, oh.

Here he was, a few miles from the nearest small town and no way to get to it, and no AAA membership to fall back on.

He went inside, got the phone book, and started to call auto parts stores. At the first one, he gave his name and address and told the woman who'd answered that he needed a battery but didn't have a way in. Another call came in, his office calling to see where he was, and by the time he'd taken care of that and switched back, the voice at the parts store was gone.

But outside, a small truck pulled up. A woman climbed out and called to him as he opened the door. "This the car with the dead

115

battery?" He nodded, not believing the woman had driven all the way out to his place.

What is more, she opened his hood and measured his dead battery. "Thought so," she said. "I'm Doris. I brought a few batteries out, but I don't have one your size. But I'll bet Fred does. Hop in."

She drove him to town, took him to a competitor's parts dealership, helped him get the right battery, and drove him back to his place and put the new battery in—the competitor's battery.

"Doris, thanks a million," Albert said. "But how do you make money like this?"

"Well, if your job depends on commuting, you're likely to need more parts or service, and where're you gonna go?"

"You have my future business. That I'll guarantee."

"That's fine. Truth is, though, that it makes me feel good, a part of things. I'll probably grab a cup of coffee on the way back and then get back to wrestling with a carburetor that needs a serious attitude adjustment."

LIVING OUTSIDE THE BOX

At every moment, we are called to make a choice. The choice is between doing what is expected of us—that's where 90 percent of the population goes, if even that—or to go far beyond what's expected and do something remarkable—something that creates conversational capital where customers rave about you to friends who, in turn, become customers. The amazing thing about stepping up to the remarkable is not only do customers feel great about you, YOU feel great about YOU.

I'm going to talk more about the spirit of giving in the next chapter. In the meantime, keep in mind that a lot of people stop at the line in the sand of their job description as if a guillotine were waiting to drop on their toes if they crossed that line. I don't mean usurp the jobs of others in your company; rather, make that effort on behalf of your customers that says you know just how they feel and what matters to them.

Think about it. When was the last time you called home and said, "Honey, you're not going to believe it. Today...I was average!" Heck no. Nobody calls home to say they did what was in their job description. You call home when you've done something great, produced monster results, and made somebody's day.

Too Good to Be True?

Bill Abemarle, a Roto Rooter truck driver in Vermont, makes calls in a truck, and in addition to the regular service of fixing septic tanks and drains, he packs along tools of his own. When he's done with any job, he takes a little extra time to clean up so wherever he has been looks as good, or better, than it was before he came. Why?

"I like to look back and say, 'I did that.' It's one thing to fix things, another to leave everyone with a good feeling. Plus, you oughtta see the letters my boss gets and the repeat business."

Beyond the Job Description

Going beyond a job description doesn't apply to salespeople at places like Nordstrom, where a salesperson is likely to wrap a package a customer bought at Macy's or even iron a customer's shirt so it can be worn that day. That chain is known for setting the highest bar, and

> Where going beyond the job description really happens is when you pitch in and help others at work, help accomplish a greater good without expecting it to be part of your evaluative performance.

front-line clerks are hired and trained with that level of above-par customer service as the signature of the store.

Where going beyond the job description really happens is when you pitch in and help others at work, help accomplish a greater good without expecting it to be part of your evaluative performance. It means being a better team member and willingly sharing the load. If you're caught up on your tasks, consider helping someone else who is crunching for a deadline.

You know what? You're going to find that instead of an extra burden, you actually feel more a part of things than ever, and that can be fun and exhilarating.

Try this:

- Find at least three things today that you can do to be remarkably helpful to a person, something that they would NEVER expect. When a thought of something to do comes to you, don't hesitate. Just do it. At the end of the day, see how you feel when you look in the mirror knowing you rocked someone's world—and *your* world at the same time.

- Listen to the needs of others. Don't turn down a chance to help someone in a jam whose priorities are clearly in the best interests of customers and the company.

- Notice that you generate a sense of self-fulfillment by doing a little extra. You'll find work far more satisfying, your relations with coworkers and customers become closer and more authentic, and you'll feel good about yourself.

chapter eighteen

Giving: Ignited Spirits Through Profound Service

> "Happiness is the only good.
> The time to be happy is now.
> The place to be happy is here.
> The way to be happy is to make others so."
>
> —Robert Green Ingersoll

Organizations have been promoting the concept of "customer satisfaction" for decades. At first blush, this sounds like a good idea, and it seems rational enough, but hey, here's a thought. If customers are *satisfied* with their service but can get a better price somewhere else, why should they stay with you?

Let's look at things from YOUR perspective: How soul-fulfilling is it for you to have yet another "satisfied" customer?

> How soul-fulfilling is it for you to have yet another "satisfied" customer?

What you really want to do with your customers—FOR them, actually—goes way beyond satisfaction. Customer success is what matters: making a lasting difference, transforming your interactions from a simple business transaction to a profound exchange between two human beings that creates a transformation of more success for the customer. This is the essence of true service.

Not that this is your only goal, but customers will pay significant premiums when they see you're making a positive difference in their lives. When you add value that improves their success and the quality of their experience, they simply won't leave.

In addition, making a positive impact on others also feeds your spirit. When you focus on something greater than yourself and concentrate on making a difference, the rewards are priceless.

LET ME TELL YOU A STORY

I know a bank teller named Mary who had a job description that said things like, "Balance the drawer every day. Greet customers. Blah, blah, blah." She read into it things that others in her job didn't.

Every week, she'd take the initiative to call at least 25 customers to ask them how they were doing. Nobody asked her, mind you. She just decided her job was to help people.

She sent notes to clients every month with information about how to manage their finances.

She kept records of the names of her customers' children and interests and asked about them when they came in. She sent clippings from the local newspaper about accomplishments of customers' children. When she met people in the grocery store, she again would ask them, "How can I do a better job for you? What's coming up I need to know so I can help you?"

She brought her own umbrellas to work that she bought at garage sales and gave them to customers when it was raining, simply saying, "Just bring it back the next time you come in."

At Christmas, Mary received 53 physical gifts that people brought to the bank for her. Not cards. GIFTS. Mary's giving spirit caused her to be the ultimate receiver.

Can you imagine how different Mary's world would be if she just stuck to her "job description?" Do you suppose she'd have as much fun? Be as valuable to the business? Get as good a bonus or salary increase? Feel as good about herself? Think about it.

Wayne W. Dyer, author of *There's a Spiritual Solution to Every Problem*, says you absolutely can't be depressed when you're being kind to others.

Here's proof. Think about the last day you were in a funk. Yes, the one you spent all day in your pajamas on the sofa wailing about how unfair life is.

Maybe you were thinking about your Dad who is a mathematician, your Mom who is a doctor, and your brother who is a physicist—and then there's little old you, who likes to color. Life just hasn't turned out the way you had hoped.

Now, if I may be so bold, it wasn't just your pajamas you were wrapped up in that day—who were you thinking about? That's right. Poor pitiful YOU! Yes, I've been there, too. It's easy to feel miserable when you focus on your problems. How could you not?

It is simply impossible to be gloomy when you turn your focus toward helping others. Being of service is the ultimate antidote you can give yourself when you're down—and you don't need a prescription. Not only do others benefit when you reach out, you do too, big time!

> **It is simply impossible to be gloomy when you turn your focus toward helping others.**

Wallace Wattles, author of *The Science of Getting Rich*, talks about the Ten Times Multiplier. His theory is that if you give 10 times more value to a customer than you collect in cash, customers will beat a path to your door.

Giving "value" doesn't mean it has to cost more. The added value you offer could be advice. It could be a system for staying in touch and providing continuing support. It could be ongoing education you give your clients by sending articles or newsletters. It could be as simple as asking customers about their needs, listening carefully, and thinking about how to fully meet those needs before you suggest a solution.

There are two kinds of people in life and business—givers and takers.

Givers are always finding ways to make an impact on others. They give freely so that they can help make their team look good and accomplish great things. They focus on making a difference through their work.

Then there are the takers. They're the ones who ask in a first interview how much vacation they will receive. They push the limits to see how little effort they can get away with. They worry about giving more value than the required hours and job description demands. They complain and find fault, often saying things like "It's not my job." "Nobody told me." "What's in it for me?"

In his insightful book, *Influence: The Psychology of Persuasion*, Robert Cialdini discusses the power of reciprocity. He believes that when you give to another, it creates a powerful and insatiable need in that person to give back. So when you give to your customers, they will reward you by buying more, bringing more business, giving more compliments, paying you more money, and sending more referrals.

Be mindful that there is a spiritual lesson here. If you give in the spirit of manipulation, or only with the intent of getting or gaining an advantage (which is, of course, the position of the taker), it could backfire. Spiritual principles are at work all the time, and violations of the giving principle can create "bad karma."

> Be a giver because it *feels* good for both parties, because it's a joy to light up someone's life, even momentarily, and the returns will naturally come back to you.

Be a giver because it *feels* good for both parties, because it's a joy to light up someone's life, even momentarily, and the returns will naturally come back to you.

Life gives to the givers and takes from the takers, and the world has a perfect accounting system.

Sometimes it's mind-boggling how simple life can be once we get out of our own way. Consider how much energy the takers expend in their attempts to protect their own interests. It takes more energy to complain about not getting a raise than to deserve one. Then think about how effortless life seems for the givers of the world, the people who regard life as an endless opportunity to make a difference. It's that tenfold principle doing its work.

HAVE I TOLD YOU LATELY THAT YOU'RE DOING A GOOD JOB, ROGER?

Roger headed down the hall toward the company auditorium, the same place he'd had his kick-off session not so long ago. He didn't know why they needed such a big space. He was just going to go over the quarterly numbers with the leadership team. But he had started this way a little early, excited to hear what he hoped, even expected, would be good news.

When he swung open the door, the place still looked as dark as three feet up inside a coal-burning chimney. He reached and flipped the nearest light switch. As if that had been a signal, people popped up from behind the chairs and yelled and screamed. They wore party hats. On the stage, a marching band started to play, and a banner across the top read "The Best Boss Ever!"

He felt stunned, not near-heart attack stunned, but a joyous numb as he looked at all the smiling faces and waving arms. Members of the Hoopla Team wheeled an enormous cake out to the front of the stage on a long cart covered with lunch meats, salmon, crusty rolls, salads, pineapples, and a festive array of other treats.

Roger caught the eye of Fredda Angle, the CFO. He waved her close.

"I take it the numbers are good?" he said.

"You betcha."

"How in the world did you manage a marching band?"

"Hefty contribution to their new uniform fund. No problem, though. We can afford it. We could spring for quite a few sets of uniforms."

"Well, this is certainly better than those talks about down-sizing we had not so long ago."

"You can say that again, Roger. Now come along. As the guest of honor, I think you should lead the way in this particular celebration."

Try this:

- Find at least 10 ways to give 10 times more value today. Yes. Today. Give and give freely. Give of your time. Give extra help. Give more to your customers than they expect. Give to your coworkers, your boss, your spouse, your friends and loved ones, and even strangers. Give until it feels good. Give with no intention of receiving.

- Experiment with the giving and serving approach for one week and keep a record of what you've given. At the end of the week, ask yourself, "Do I feel better?" "Do the people around me feel better?" "Have I made a difference?" "Do I see that I'm receiving more than ever before?" If you like the result, plan to do it again the next week, and the next, and the next.

- Don't even THINK of leaving a dirty dish in the company kitchen. How you do anything is how you do everything. You will be perceived as a slacker who needs others to take care of you instead of a contributor! That's right. Your mother doesn't work here.

- Challenge yourself to *never* again complain that someone isn't noticing your contributions enough, "He has the same job title but he's doing half the work." "She didn't even get 50 mailings out last week." "I just did all the work, and he got all the credit." There is one thing you can count on. If you're adding massive value, others will notice, and you will get be rewarded. IF, however, you do it for that reason, it won't work nearly so well. And IF you are whiny and complaining that you're not being recognized or didn't get enough of yours, you will be perceived to be a whiner, and all your good efforts will be viewed as a selfish attempt to self-promote instead of a sincere contribution. Bring your best self to work everyday. That self is selfless.

PART IV

Obstacles...
or Minor Speed Bumps?
Clear the Road Blocks
and Saboteurs:
Ground Rules to Keep
Dark Moments in the Past
from Poisoning the
Glorious Future

chapter nineteen

What We Have Here Is a Failure to Communicate... Clearly

"Good communication is as stimulating as black coffee, and just as hard to sleep after."

—Anne Morrow Lindbergh

You need to use powerful and positive language about what you will do and the attitude you expect from others.

PROBLEMS OR OPPORTUNITIES?

Any management team will always have problems. There's nothing new or different in that. In fact, if you don't want problems, don't be a leader. The problem is when you identify each problem as a problem. When you do that, it often becomes one of the problems you revisit every week, and it becomes a part of the "same old, same old." Sound familiar?

Every time you call problems "problems," you stop all ability to resolve them. Why? Because you can't get what you want by focusing on what you don't want. You don't want the problem, but you focus on it, so it tends to persist. If you restate the "problem" as an opportunity, then you are focusing on what you do want, and you will start moving toward it.

At one company, I got them to set the ground rule to never call their problems "problems" again, but to call them "opportunities for a breakthrough." When they did, everything changed. For each roadblock in their path, they forced themselves to create a list of strategies to break through to the opportunity. When they chose the best strategy, they made a person accountable to make it happen, set a deadline, and gave it a budget if necessary.

Hmmm, suddenly there were no problems.

There were new opportunities every week as a result of seizing their opportunities. Their profits increased 44 percent within six months—which, of course, increased the quality of the "opportunities."

Welcome Feedback

Jack has filed for bankruptcy three times. He's a nice guy. In every one of his businesses, his vendors offered suggestions to help him. He met every suggestion with a comment about what THEY didn't understand. His managers had ideas for getting more business. He knew better and told them why they were wrong. They had ideas on how to bring down expenses. He knew better and didn't listen to what they had to say. Of course, he never implemented the ideas to bring down expenses.

> Every time you call problems "problems," you stop all ability to resolve them.

His wife had a few ideas. Of course, she didn't run the business, so what did she know? Even his kids had a few ideas because they worked in the business. But, hey, they were kids. They didn't have his 20 years of business experience.

While he did his third bankruptcy, he went through his fourth divorce. No accident. The only opinion that mattered was his.

He never made it go. He worked every day after age 62. He had to. There was no money for groceries. When he couldn't work anymore, he moved in with his oldest daughter to be supported. Of course, he wouldn't listen to his doctor to take his meds. He died at age 65 with no friends, no money, and a distant relationship with his children.

The point is, when you get feedback, it is because someone cares. Consider at least one percent of what that person has to say as being extremely valuable and say to the person sharing, "Thank you, I'll consider this..." but never reject them.

Be Open to Feedback and Change

"Lester is a little off" is how they described him. He had been on the board for years, and during those years, he rarely missed a day where he would come into the company and, in front of customers, yell at employees. "Not exactly a motivator" is how they described it with a chuckle.

"If you can crack him, you can crack anything."

As a team, we agreed on our code of how we treat each other. We agreed to "No gossip. No excuses. No stories. No blaming. State everything in the positive."

> **As a team, we agreed on our code of how we treat each other. We agreed to "No gossip. No excuses. No stories. No blaming."**

Bingo. That one hit.

Lester had never stated a request in the positive. In fact, the only things he ever said were negative and demoralizing. It's not that once in a while we don't all need a little kick in the pants with a solid request that says, "Get moving…you're not getting it." But his typewriter of commands only had one letter on it, and it wasn't working.

They had just accepted him as being a little nuts. When customers commented, the team members would just say, "He's just a little different—don't worry about him."

At a session, when the team all agreed to live the commitments with integrity and call each other tight no matter if the receptionist had to camp at the CEO's feet until she heard the request for a change of behavior, the agreement was that every person would call each other person on their behaviors, and they would all live by the rules of how to treat each other.

Near the end of the evening Lester stood up and said, "Where were you 40 years ago when I needed you?" He got it. He now knew that he simply misunderstood some of the assumed rules of life that people who work in and run extraordinary organizations and those who manage great families understand. And now he understood. And the whole town was talking of his transformation—and for the first time in decades, his smile beamed.

Tell Me the Good News, Tell Me the Bad News, But Don't Surprise Me— Keeping Your Team Posted

Samantha was supposed to be in charge of making sure that all the registrations were confirmed with clients on time. But she had a problem. A big problem. The problem was with getting the registrations out through the Internet because—you guessed it—there seemed to be a (technical) problem. She called the web expert to fix it. He said it would take a week. She decided to wait to send out the registrations, even though the company standard was that all registrations were out within 24 hours of accepting payment. She didn't tell anyone else on her team or her boss about her decision. Five days later, the company's largest client called to complain to the CEO. The CEO said he couldn't believe that could have happened because they had "a standard." Now they were all surprised.

Try this:

- Go to the people you work with and live with and let them know that being human has limitations for you, too. When they're giving you suggestions that they feel would be very helpful, you are likely to deflect their ideas to protect your status quo; let them know that you would like them to not let you get away with it by saying something like, "Please consider this and get back to me tomorrow if you think this idea has some merit."

- When other people are defensive to feedback that you think would be helpful for them to hear, simply say, "I'd love for you to hear what I have to say, even if you think it's wrong at this time. I'm sure some part of it is and some part or parts might be right, and I'd love you to consider my ideas for a full day before letting me know what you think."

- Next time you hit an obstacle, instead of saying, "You have GOT to be kidding," say, "Hmmmm. There has to be an opportunity here someplace. This is happening for some perfect reason. I look forward to finding out what that is." Another way to approach this is to look for the blessing in every situation. This can sometimes seem like a bizarre idea at first. On the other hand, people who have adopted this practice find that it's life-changing.

- Consider how honest and clear communication can clear up perceived problems or obstacles.

chapter twenty

Vanish the Energy Vampires

"They are Vampires, and their modus operandi is not to steal your blood but rather, your precious energy. Your life-force. Your mojo. To drain you emotionally and psychologically. To frustrate you with their repetitious, self-indulgent, attention-seeking diatribe."

—Craig Harper

When Blanche Springer comes into any room in the building where she works, people flinch. They don't reach for wooden stakes, or silver bullets, or strings of garlic for the neck, but a few of them do suspect Blanche has a coffin of Transylvania dirt down in the basement boiler room. Why? Because Blanche is an energy vampire.

She doesn't wear all black, and you can even see her reflection in mirrors. Yet her coworkers know she is a vampire as soon as they open their mouths.

"I'm up for a promotion. Isn't that great?"

Blanche: "You'll still be sucking wind with your sister. She's a doctor, isn't she?"

"Sales are going to be up, up, up this year."

Blanche: "That's only because they were in the toilet last year."

"My glass is half full."

Blanche: "You call that a glass?"

Have you noticed how easily some people suck you dry of all your life force? Within seconds, they can

Have you noticed how easily some people suck you dry of all your life force?

take your great day and make it miserable. Blanche is an idea stomper and represents just one of the types of behaviors that suck you dry. What should you do when you encounter them to "protect your bloood."

You've been to meetings where one person criticizes everyone's ideas but has no useful replacement ideas of their own. Get out the transfusion bags because several people have just had their blood and energy sucked away during what could have been a productive meeting.

You Think You've Got it Bad...

Another energy drain comes from "perpetual victims," the folks who are always talking about what the world did to them.

Alexis Olans is one. She has been divorced for 28 years and still daily blames "that S.O.B. who RUINED my LIFE!" And she falsely feels that he's *still* at the center of other conspiracies against her having any joy in her life. She can *never* put any slight or injury behind her.

Onlookers have no difficulty in figuring out who *really* ruined Alexis' life. *She* did. She did it by not moving on and by choosing to stay miserable, which kept all other marriage prospects far away.

There's a reason that victims remain victims. They receive feedback that supports their victimhood by others who are often well-meaning but unconscious of the negative impact.

> There's a reason that victims remain victims. They receive feedback that supports their victimhood by others who are often well-meaning but unconscious of the negative impact.

When "perpetual victims" complain about how awful their lives are, their supporters, usually other victims, support them by buying into it. "Yep," they'll say, "Ain't it just *awful*." That's all the positive reinforcement the victim needs, as off they go seeking the next hit of

"Oh, you poor thing" from another person. They thrive on all this attention. It feeds their need. The problem is that if that person ever went to the center of the universe, they'd be shocked to see they're not in it.

A person who supports a victim in that way is not really a friend. This kind of supporter is as toxic as the victim herself. Sane people distance themselves from victims.

So what do you do when a victim comes to you and complains yet again about something someone else or some other department did? Easy. Place accountability for change back on that person.

Simply use this phrase over and over again until you get results. "Sounds like a problem, an opportunity really. What are YOU going to do to make sure that doesn't happen again or to become at peace with it so you can move on?"

Victims hate that. They either have to stop being a victim or stop draining your energy, or they find someone else who is a willing enabler to victimhood. Either way, you win!

If they go on telling you why it's not them at all and that the other party is the guilty one, listen for only a moment—and then, when you can get a word in edgewise, repeat the mantra, "Sounds like a problem. You're pretty powerful, so I know you don't view yourself as a victim. Tell me what you're doing to make the situation better."

Sometimes it takes a broken record to get the message through. Imagine you're trying to drive home a point to a teenager. It may take a few times.

One of two things will happen. Ideally, the complainer will go fix the problem at the source. The next-best scenario is that they leave you the heck alone, knowing you are not going to support their victimhood. This enables you to have a safe work environment, free from those who hang on you like a torch singer on a microphone, singing endless refrains of the Pity-Me Blues.

Whiners

Joe Hassel, the been-here-too-long programmer, as perceived by his teammates, hasn't had a joyful day in over a decade. According to him, "Our customers are so dumb, they can't figure out how to use our systems on their own." Instead of advancing the situation by saying something like, "We need to do a better job of helping our clients adapt to our systems once we finish our installations. I'd suggest we offer them an online manual."

How helpful is it to criticize without a realistic solution? It's maybe as constructive as buying a box of caramels for a friend who complains about having a loose filling.

Whiners aren't *trying* to be helpful. It's not their nature to *help*.

Whiners aren't *trying* to be helpful. It's not their nature to *help*. Whiners are first cousins of the victim types. They're better at finding fault than figuring out a solution.

Ah, whiners. Whiners have the capacity to suck possibilities out of a situation faster than Count Dracula can grab a quick snack.

Instead of telling you what *can* be done, whiners spend hours vividly outlining what *can't* be done and why. Had whiners ruled the world, we'd still be sitting in our caves, huddled around the fire complaining that we can't find the remote control.

Whining is an attempt to "one-up" others by dismissing all possibilities before anyone has a chance to make a suggestion. Oddly enough, while a whiner's statement may sound definite, the bluster is actually born of insecurity. Although they have enough mental sharpness to point out problems, they don't have enough confidence to work at resolving them.

Many people who grow up to be whiners learned early on in life that they could get more attention by voicing a complaint than by trying to correct a situation.

There isn't much room for someone like that in a workplace where team members want to "rock" or in an office where everyone is willing to carry their weight and then some.

Of course, this is not to say that there will never be any whining again, ever. Sometimes it goes with the human condition.

And if we're honest with ourselves, we have to admit that we've ALL have had our moments of whining. We all have our occasional pity parties or bouts of attention seeking.

Despite our knowing how whining can negatively impact others and render us ineffective, there's a remote chance we might once again choose to grab for that taste of whine. We're only human.

Although the ugly truth is that there's nothing attractive about whining; the only beauty is in knowing there are ways to prevent and avoid the condition.

Here's one sure cure: Ask your family, friends, and coworkers to give you a signal the next time you start to whine, moan, or groan. Ask them to make a "W" with three fingers as a reminder to stop whining and start creating a solution.

When you get the sign…stop IMMEDIATELY and laugh at yourself for having had a "moment." Remind yourself how good it feels to figure out what you can and will do about a challenging situation instead of simply letting yourself circle the drain.

There's a feeling in our culture that we're all in this alone. Give yourself permission to create a safety net of those who care about you so they can lend a hand when you're working on self-improvement.

The resourcefulness of energy vampires is unlimited with rolling eyes, arms crossed, smirks, whining, victimhood…you name it. You know it when you see it, or should I say "feel it," as you are sucked dry. Whatever the form, know that you have the right to protect yourself and invite that person to get it or get on.

Try this:

- Whenever something happens that is not to your liking, ask yourself what you did to create the situation. Learn from that so you don't repeat the situation.

- Make energy vampires accountable to themselves. Don't encourage that kind of behavior with positive attention.

- Do everything to avoid victims. If using the lines listed previously don't work, do what you can to steer clear of the person so that you can preserve your energy.

- If the person is part of your responsibility, then it's up to you to convert the person or join the mob with pitchforks and torches and get that person out of the company before their toxic behavior spreads and you have a company full of the walking dead.

chapter twenty-one

Bust the Baditudes

"The only disability in life is a bad attitude."

—Scott Hamilton

"What do you want?"

That's how the receptionist answered the phone, in that tone of "How dare you take my time from me." You were an intruder in her world, not a welcome participant. That was Carol Shively, about whom quite a few people had called the accounting firm's president to tell him she was without peer as "The World's Worst Receptionist."

Television sitcoms are filled with cranky, even "techy" employees who add humor to a script because they are funny in context of the people tensions that have to exist to make a show entertaining. People like that aren't such a chuckle in real life. Carol, for instance, had inspired coworkers to fantasize about slipping mood enhancers into her coffee.

Not surprisingly, the numbers were down at the accounting firm. It was not doing well, floundering, in fact, and Carol epitomized the company's entire environment and dwindling results—in fact, she was a key source. When the president was asked about Carol, he was quick to agree that she was a real party pooper, but she'd been with the company for 20 years, and they were just counting the years until her retirement.

When the company went through the steps to become a happier and more motivated workplace, the president himself was as surprised as anyone when he got a call telling him that the company's receptionist was the best receptionist he had ever encountered.

"Our Carol?" he said. "Do you mean her?"

Yes, it was the same "Carol" who had held the title as the world's worst receptionist. A coworker had THE conversation with her. And because of that, she'd made a total flip-flop, and for the best; the company's results began to reflect the improved environment with an upward swing of numbers that matched the upward tugs at the corners of the president's new smile. And what was the conversation? Well—read on.

There's always one—one in every club, every workplace, every school. There always seems to be at least one person who just doesn't want to be there. They're usually masters of passive-aggressive behavior. They make noises of disgust, contort their faces to show contempt— and if that doesn't do it, they get loud and physical by shoving a few things around while doing the other two. Blend this with a few eye rolls, and yes, you have a pain in the butt acting like a spoiled child film star.

Some people are absolutely tireless in their drive to contaminate the rest of their team.

> **Some people are absolutely tireless in their drive to contaminate the rest of their team.**

Here's the thing about people who don't want to be there—they shouldn't be! Life is too short to be at a place where they aren't thriving. Life isn't a dress rehearsal.

Sometimes it has nothing to do with the place, the situation, or the other people involved. It's often the case that relentlessly unhappy people don't want to be *anywhere* with *themselves*. Such people might leave your company, go elsewhere, and be miserable at the next place, and the next, and…. Remember, *wherever you go, there you are.*

They don't understand that they are the problem, of course. They believe they are victims of circumstance. They think others are being unfair to them.

Right there is the core of the problem—it's all about *them*. Unhappy people are focused squarely on what the world, the boss, their coworkers, the Pope, isn't giving *them*. They don't know that their unhappiness would go away if *they* would focus *outward* on making a difference.

WHAT'S ROGER UP TO NOW?

It was Saturday, so there should be no noises coming from the auditorium. Roger poked his head inside the door and had a look around. Lawrence Gaines, the maintenance man, had a rag in one hand and a bottle of Murphy Oil Soap in the other. He rubbed hard at the wooden arm rests of each seat until they gleamed.

"It's your day off, Lawrence. Why aren't you home watching football or something?" Roger said. He knew all too well that Lawrence was the company's biggest crabapple. No one had ever seen him smile, but they'd seen him scowl or mutter curses to himself as he went around the company halls like a storm cloud brewing up lightning and thunder. His mood was so legendary that when he snapped at a group of other employees, they had gotten back at him by putting an advertisement in the local paper: "Strawberries, 25 cents a quart." They'd put his phone number in the ad. His phone had rung so steadily the next day that they heard he'd torn it off the wall and hurled it to smash into pieces.

Right after his kick-off meeting, Roger had sat in when Lawrence's supervisor had given him the talk. That's where you say, "I'm so excited about where this team is going. I could be wrong, but my sense is that you don't share the excitement, and that's okay. If this isn't your thing, you have to go find your thing."

Roger hadn't been sure which way Lawrence would go, but he had stayed. Not only that, he smiled more and occasionally brought in boxes of doughnuts purchased out of his own pocket to put in the break room.

Now he grinned like a kid caught in the candy jar and looked up from the wood he was rubbing until it shined. "I heard there was going to be an awards ceremony in here tomorrow for those Special Olympics kids. I wasn't happy with how clean the place looked, so I came in to give it a little extra-special touching up."

"I have just one thing to say to you," Roger said. "What did you do with the Lawrence we used to have?"

So here's a conversation you can have with any person who displays an "attitude" on their sleeve. You don't need to be the boss or even in the same department with this person to have the conversation. It is extremely direct yet exceptionally loving because it demonstrates that you care enough to get them to make a choice—between bringing their whole heart to their current situation or going to find a new situation that makes them happy.

The conversation may only take about 15 seconds, tops, but has transformed a lot of people from being miserable blamers to on-fire contributors. And the beauty is that it works in an instant.

There are four parts to the conversation—and you don't want to miss any part:

1. "I'm so excited about where our team is going." (*Let them know the team is going with or without them. Their dramatic scenes to try to get others to join them in misery are to no avail because the team IS moving ahead.*)

2. "And I could be wrong, but my sense is that you don't share that excitement." (*Don't give any reasons. Just state that you have an intuitive feeling. If you get into the reasons, you're asking for a tug-of-war that goes nowhere.*)

3. "And that's okay." (*This is where the freedom comes in. They see you're okay with either decision. They can be in, or they can be out. All you're saying is that they have a choice. It takes away their ability to put up a fuss and get defensive with you.*)

4. "Because maybe this isn't your thing. But if this isn't your thing, you need to go find your thing!" (*Ouch! That put the responsibility for a decision squarely on their shoulders. "Get in or get out—you decide."*)

So the whole thing should sound like this, without a breath:

"I'm so excited about where our team is going. I could be wrong, but my sense is you don't share that excitement. And that's okay. Because maybe this *isn't* your thing. But if this isn't your thing, you need to go *find* your thing!"

The reason you don't want to breathe is you don't want them to have a chance to interrupt with, "Why do you say that?" or "Who told you what?" or "You're wrong…it's just that THIS place…."

And then ask them to make a decision within 24 hours because their life is wasting away without that decision. Ask if you can meet the next day to hear their decision.

Do NOT allow them to avoid the decision!

If you're thinking your boss or coworker needs to hear this, no problem. You can have this conversation at any level. It's just about caring enough about the person to help them make good decisions.

Here's the funny (amazing, really) thing. Ninety percent of the time, the bad apple person says, "You're right. I've been a jerk"—and that person then becomes a star performer because the boundless energy she was using to manipulate her coworkers into joining her in her misery is now channeled to productive use.

As for the other 10 percent—well, as one CEO put it when he finally had to hand the pink slip to an unrepentant bad apple worker, the coworkers of that "attitude queen" made picket signs the day she left that said, "Yay, yay, the wicked witch is dead!" And company performance went up immediately!

> The coworkers of that "attitude queen" made picket signs the day she left that said, "Yay, yay, the wicked witch is dead!"

It happens often. If a person who chooses to leave after "the conversation" was one of the top performers or even the top performer, the team that remains immediately picks up the slack of the newly departed, and results rise to a higher level. The reason is clear: They can perform infinitely better without having to live in a toxic waste dump of "attitude."

We've all needed others to give us the conversation at one point or another. There is nothing more loving than for someone who cares about us to give us the "get over it" conversation so we can "get on with it." Just make sure you come from a place of caring instead of a place of anger. That will make all the difference. Most people with an attitude just want to know that someone wants them to make a good choice.

Try this:

- Have "the conversation" whenever you feel like someone is emotionally checked out. That's where you say, "I'm so excited about where this team is going. I could be wrong, but my sense is that you don't share the excitement, and that's okay. If this isn't your thing, you have to go find your thing." We ALL need "the conversation" at some time or another. Do it with kindness and care in your heart. If you're angry, chill out first. Remember, the point is to guide them to make a decision of greatness, not to push them.

chapter twenty-two

Better Off Somewhere Else?
Get On the Happy Bus...or
Get Off the Bus

"You don't have to go home, but you can't stay here."

—Mike Blakely, "Closing Time" song

Julie was a pile person. Her office was scattered with big and small piles of papers, files, and magazine articles she had clipped to read later. Each pile represented a different project. Each project was late. Piles are procrastination. Piles are frustrating. Piles remind you that you have a terrible time when it comes to hitting the ground and running. No surprise, then, when Julie couldn't complete her projects on time.

One day, her boss said, "I don't care how you do it, but it's time to change your habits. I can't have more of your projects delayed. I can't have you miss any more deadlines. When you do, it leads to a chain reaction down the line. It makes you look bad, and worse, it makes me look bad."

So did Julie take the advice? Hardly. She announced to her work team that she was going to go back to school. "I'm leaving the company in a month for a great opportunity," she said. Her field of study? "Botany." Something she always wanted to study.

Can you relate? Is that you or someone who reports to you? Think about it and look at another similar scenario.

Casey at the Bat

Casey, a two-year management trainee, had started off with the ambition of a presidential candidate. He was going places, and he let people know it. But then the real world intruded. Work was a lot harder than he imagined. When it came time for his annual review, it was no surprise to anyone—except maybe to him—that he scored very poorly on his quality of work. "Your analytical skills need to align properly with your workload," his boss had written.

So did Casey go back to the drawing board and rethink his work habits? Hardly. He cut and ran. A few weeks later, he posted his resume on the Internet. Then he announced his resignation. He bragged to his coworkers that he had found an even better opportunity, one that he could scarcely afford to pass up.

Is Casey really a winner? Did he listen...and hear? Or did he head for the exit light?

Up to Andrea

Andrea, a translation specialist, had a reputation around the office. Her nickname was "The Troublemaker" because of her repeated run-ins with her coworkers. In her mind, they were all jerks and losers. Rude and untrustworthy. Backstabbers and villains. Gossip was her tool of choice. Hurt feelings were the angel dust she spread everywhere.

After months of repeated run-ins, she figured out a way to solve her reign of unpopularity. Andrea resigned, she told everyone, to "travel to exotic places." "It was something," she said with a snooty little smile, "that I always wanted to do."

In all of these cases, each took the *Shortcut to Nowhere—the Express Train*. It came time for their company to firm up expectations and the employee to decide if he or she wanted to comply or fly.

Maybe it sounds like "my way or the highway" to an employee. It shouldn't if it is handled with grace and dignity. But perception can be everything, particularly to someone who already thinks he or she knows everything.

Sociologists like to talk about the trait in early mankind to fight or flee. It's right up there with hunters and gatherers. Are you giving yourself and your company a fair chance, or is it just easier to flee?

> Perception can be everything, particularly to someone who already thinks he or she knows everything.

Managers have to think about whether they are communicating as clearly as they should. Are they making the options to stay and merge as part of a "killer app" team as attractive as they can be? Employees have to consider another whole array of possibilities, among which are a resume that looks like a patchwork quilt, the consistent loss of friends, a path of denial, and pitching a spin to themselves that they are better off.

In the end, both parties are losers, but the company is likely to go on and quickly refill its ranks. So you figure out who really takes the spill in this situation.

Try this:

- If the problem person is you, or someone who reports to you, have the frank and open kind of conversation that includes the person staying and making the workplace better. If you need to use a mirror to have this conversation, you're going to have to struggle twice as hard to get past denial.

- Get the person to admit to both the problem and to help draft the reasonable solution.

- If the person is unsalvageable and impenetrable with your coaching, then count your blessings and recruit what your team really needs.

- If you decide to leave because you've done your very best to put your big girl or big boy pants on and address the situation with finesse and care and it didn't work, then know you made a good decision as well. Just make sure you're not being delusional about having done your best.

chapter twenty-three

Gossip:
The Hurt That Never Heals

"Gossip needn't be false to be evil—there's a lot of truth that shouldn't be passed around."

—Frank A. Clark

"Did you see Stanley's car? That red Corvette he's been so proud of. Someone's taken a key and let his paint job have it good. Looks like whoever did it started to spell a bad word, too. Do you think Stanley's been catting around where he shouldn't and got caught?"

"Yeah, likely some jealous husband did it."

Stanley, a mousy-looking accountant with a slight middle-age spread and a receding hairline hears through the grapevine later that day that he's the biggest rake in the company. A couple of female coworkers sneer at him, and one gives him a come-hither look that is equally unwelcome. He gets back on the phone with the body shop and tells them how he sideswiped a bush coming out of his drive.

He hangs up, and people are giving still him the eye, and a couple people suppress snickers when he attends an afternoon meeting. He finds he is getting far less done than usual, and he wonders how these rumors got started.

There is nothing more violent and violating in an organization than gossip. You may as well swing baseball bats at each other. At least the physical damage can be repaired. The emotional damage done by

> There is nothing more violent and violating in an organization than gossip. You may as well swing baseball bats at each other.

gossip destroys trust, and without trust, there is no reason for a relationship. All within earshot are damaged.

Our thirst for gossip is apparently not quenched by the tabloids—otherwise, why would we bring so much of it into the workplace?

No good comes from it. Here's how it goes.

Pat has a problem with Terry. No big deal. When you work with people, you will have problems. (Remember the study where they crammed rats into a small space? Wasn't pretty.) So what does Pat do? He tells Michelle, and Betty, and Joe. And Jim. AND Sherri.

There. Handled. Now we have complete and total chaos.

In the unlikely event he has any sense of decency, Pat will feel like a loser three minutes later because he just acted like a two-year-old in front of five of his peers. But he probably doesn't know that. This is normal behavior for him. Remember, he was the kid who shaved off his cousin's eyebrows while he was sleeping. His cousin looked surprised for three months. And Pat's peers most likely feel a tad dirty because they were contributors in the gossip. They've just proven they can't be trusted to handle things directly and didn't have the emotional fortitude to deflect the conversation and stay out of it.

It gets even better. Pat quickly realizes he can't trust Michelle, Betty, Joe, Jim, or Sherri. They are the kind of people who welcome gossip, you see, and people who accept gossip tend to be equal-opportunity mudslingers. Soon enough, they'll be welcoming gossip about Pat.

Michelle, Betty, Joe, Jim, and Sherri figure it's just a matter of time before Pat will be gossiping about each of them. And they're right. And Terry surely knows at some level that something is going on and has a sense he can't trust any of them.

Okay everybody, on the count of three—*be happy and productive*!

If you want an organization or family that functions, every person must be 100 percent accountable for creating a safe environment, and it's not safe if you allow gossip. It is emotionally debilitating to be in an environment where people are free to talk behind your back.

So again—forgive yourself for *everything*. What's past is past. Nobody cares anymore that you put decaf in the coffeemaker for three weeks and then switched to espresso. Besides, the last time we had any formal training in conflict resolution was in the fourth grade.

For now, start fresh. Vow that you will NEVER, EVER talk behind another person's back.

All Pat had to do was to go to Terry and say, "Dude, when you are late with that report, I have to go on my knees to my boss because I'm late. Please promise me you'll get that report to me on time from now on."

Done. That's it. It's just that easy.

You won't win the Oscar for Drama Queen by tsking, rolling your eyes, making sounds of disgust, and otherwise showing signs of misery trying to win others over to your side. Have you ever seen that technique work? That's just fine. There are much better awards to be won—and you get to keep your dignity while those around you keep their self-respect. Now that's something you can thank the Academy for.

Gossip isn't made any more acceptable when you begin with, "I really shouldn't be telling you this, but…."

If someone comes to you with gossip, simply say, "Gee, it sounds like you need to talk to Terry directly so you can work this out." Repeat that until the person gives up and wakes up!

Incidentally, bosses are people, too. If you want to alienate yourself from your boss, just pull some of those maneuvers where you start talking with others about what your boss has done or hasn't done. "He finished your report? He didn't finish MINE!" "She probably won't give me the time off anyway." "WHAT!? He *told me*…" "I've been asking for this for *three years* and Tom *still* hasn't…" "Well, *of course* Sue likes you. You're her (eye-roll) *faaaa*-vorite. But she *hates* me."

Yep, that'll do it. Just pull that garbage around your team a few times, and the boss will find out. The great thing is you'll be able to continue this in the unemployment line: "My boss wasn't fair with me." Who knows—maybe you'll find a sympathetic audience there. But the real question is, "Who REALLY wasn't fair when you didn't treat your boss like a human being by communicating directly and honestly?"

At some point in life, we all have to grow up and live by grown-up rules. None of us was born with emotional maturity. We all have to develop it. And it begins when we ask ourselves at what age we're going to *decide*, at last, to grow up.

> **At some point in life, we all have to grow up and live by grown-up rules.**

The litmus test is this: If you say it to hurt, it's gossip. If you say it and it could hurt, it's gossip. Even if it's true, it's gossip.

People who gossip feel inferior and are trying to make someone else look more inferior to put themselves one up by being "the least worst." Guess what…we're on to you. And it doesn't work.

Now that you know how to stop gossip, a cancer that eats at the hearts and souls of the people you work with and debilitates their self-confidence, you CAN look forward to a satisfying career in a place where you can thrive.

Try this:

- Tell the people around you that you have zero tolerance for gossip.

- If anyone starts to gossip, interrupting is okay here. Simply say, "Sounds like you need to have a conversation with…"

- If you begin to gossip, stop yourself and say, "Wait a minute. This isn't right. I need to go to the other person. I apologize for hurting you by sharing something that was inappropriate. It won't happen again."

chapter twenty-four

Understanding Perspective: Always Being Right Can Be Wrong

"Confidence comes not from always being right but from not fearing to be wrong."

—Peter T. Mcintyre

Arthur Sanderson got a call at 5:30 a.m. that woke both he and his wife in their Santa Monica home. The call was from an administrative assistant in the East Coast office.

"Sorry about the time zone differences, but I'm about to send out the mail over here and just want to know if you're sure about this bid."

"Yes, I'm sure."

Arthur hung up, looked at the clock, and grumbled, "Minimum wage worker, too."

His head had barely hit the pillow when the phone rang again. It was the division manager. He got virtually the same message and responded, "I'm positive. Send it off."

He was just drifting off at last. Ring. He grabbed the phone, threw a pillow, and snapped, "What?"

It was the regional manager. This time he made it as clear as he could. If they sent off the bid Arthur had approved, it could cost the company millions. "There's a decimal point missing. Do you want to take another look at this before we send it off? Or not?"

"Oh," Arthur said in a voice slightly smaller in pitch than that of a mouse. "I'll take another look. Don't send it."

Arthur wasn't a pounder of desks or the kind of executive who would normally raise his voice. But he'd just had a refresher course in Humility 101.

At a major airline, an executive had his greatest breakthrough when he decided to visit the mechanics in the hangers to see if they had any ideas on how the company could cut costs. He'd come away with vastly more pragmatic (and valuable, it turned out) information than he'd gotten from any of his office coworkers.

At a company meeting, a woman in the crowd dissented from what a manager was pitching. He asked her to clarify what she meant, hoping to publicly shame her and thus quiet her. Turned out, though, she had a good and valid point, one that would make a huge difference. Good thing he'd listened after all.

We all like to be right. It's part of our egos. But there's such a thing as being so right you're wrong. Managers with a "my way or the highway" attitude may never learn to listen and garner feedback of the most valuable kind. You don't have to be like that—in fact, you shouldn't be.

> We all like to be right. It's part of our egos. But there's such a thing as being so right you're wrong.

Never hesitate to listen to or learn from customers, coworkers, or even people who share criticism about your company. The old, "I can't hear you," with fingers in your ears isn't going to do you much good when it turns out that your being right leads to a long-term boo-boo.

Life is a learning process, and if you don't feel an occasional sting, then you are probably tuning out precious information. No one is right all the time. So there is ALWAYS a slight chance that you're wrong. Act as though that is possible.

Try this:

- Make a list of people who may know more aspects of their job in your company than you do. Note their specialties. Call them or share a meal. Stop trying to impress and decide to be wide open to learning.

- Stop being a know-it-all and start having the opening and curiosity of a child. Not only will you learn more, but you will be more likable—even to you!

- Watch to see if you are really listening or just waiting for your chance to talk.

chapter twenty-five

Clean Up Your Messes and Mistakes: Restore Trust

> *"If you have made mistakes, there is always another chance for you. You may have a fresh start any moment you choose, for this thing we call 'failure' is not the falling down, but the staying down."*
>
> —Mary Pickford

You're human. Yes? If so, you'll make mistakes. You can count on it.

You'll miss deadlines. You'll disappoint people by not meeting their expectations and living up to your commitments.

If there are people who evolved to the point that they have complete integrity at every moment, I haven't met one yet.

Knowing that, it is critical to having great relationships that you have the ability to clean up the messes as you make them.

Ron, a marketing specialist, missed deadline after deadline, and suddenly his entire team felt let down by him and worked around him whenever they could.

Sharon, a loan processor, made mistakes in the loan documents repeatedly. Nobody even closed a loan without having to spend a great deal of extra time checking her work. Sharon couldn't figure out why she wasn't being advanced or earning bonuses because she had been there longer.

Tim, a teenager, told his mom he'd weed the flower garden every week during the summer as a contribution to the family. More weeks than not, the dandelions outnumbered the daisies.

All of these things, in the viewpoint of Ron, Sharon, and Tim, weren't very big things. Heck, they did many things well.

What each of them missed is that they consistently defiled the trust of the people around them, and relationships are built on trust. Without that foundation, there is no basis for a relationship.

What each of them didn't understand is that they breached the trust each time they didn't do what they said they would do. And each didn't come back to "clean up the mess."

> A clean-up has two parts—acknowledging the result wasn't okay and committing to take corrective action.

A clean-up has two parts—acknowledging the result wasn't okay and committing to take corrective action.

So when Ron missed a deadline, he owed it to his team to go to them and say, "I'm so sorry I missed that deadline. There's no excuse. It shouldn't have happened. I'm putting a tickler system in place to remind myself earlier in the process so it won't happen again."

Sharon could say to her boss, "I can see that I made mistakes in this document, and I *know* that's not acceptable. I will put a reminder at my desk to checklist each document before I submit it to make sure I have checked that each document is accurate. I want you to be able to trust me."

Tim can clean up things with his parents by saying, "I blew it. I know we had a deal, and I didn't follow through. That's not okay with me either because I want you to know you can always trust me. I'm going to set a deadline that I have to always have the garden weeded by Saturday afternoon at 2:00."

People make mistakes. We always will. And others will forgive us for everything if we simply come clean and show we *know* we were out of integrity and that we care enough to fix the situation.

When we don't, not only do others lose faith in us—*we* lose faith in ourselves. Every agreement that isn't followed through weakens our own self-esteem. The self-esteem downward spiral, once begun, leads to more unkept promises and even worse self-esteem.

> People make mistakes. We always will. And others will forgive us for everything if we simply come clean and show we know we were out of integrity and that we care enough to fix the situation.

A short message of, "I blew it, and it isn't okay. Here's what I'll do to correct it," is all people need to hear to restore faith in us and to have us restore faith in ourselves.

Try this:

- Make a list of all the people that are impacted by an obligation that you didn't fulfill recently. Contact each to let them know you blew it, and it isn't okay, and you're taking corrective action.

- If someone doesn't forgive you or responds with, "Yep, that was a bummer, but that's okay, and I'm glad I brought it up," know that you still did your part in cleaning up the mess. You're not responsible for another person's reaction.

One Last Thing

"Don't let what you cannot do interfere with what you can do."

—Coach John Wooden

It is hard, impossible some said, to get all of a really big idea into a small book. I end up leaving out raw emotion, moments when faces light up when people realize that life is very likely to be quite different from here forward. I struggle to describe how a really big ship at sea slowly starts to change course, and then makes better time than ever. I paint the picture, but a glance at the bottom line of a spreadsheet in a few weeks is really what is going to have the CEO grinning like the circus baboon.

But, in the end, you have a motivated workplace that is more human, with people nurturing each other, celebrating each other's successes. The really big idea is essentially a simple one: Identify, encourage, and emphasize the positive;

> In the end, you have a motivated workplace that is more human, with people nurturing each other, celebrating each other's successes.

and identify, discourage, and banish the negative. Simple, but not easy. It takes an initial leap and persistent follow-up. I hope I've shared a process that can work for you.

> Once everyone is committed to the transformation vision, you will all experience the benefits: at work, with your customers, at home. You will prosper.

Anyone can get the ball rolling. Once everyone is committed to the transformation vision, you will all experience the benefits: at work, with your customers, at home. You will prosper. Your business will prosper. When you feel that swell in your chest and you really do look forward to going to work most of the time, then you'll be in a far, far better place than you may be today. I wish you the best of success at getting to that place. May all your days ahead be full of cheers, high fives, and the loftiest results you can imagine.

WHERE THE HECK IS ROGER?

The sun beamed up at him from the rippling surface of the pool, so he slipped his sunglasses back on and reached for the tall sweating glass of piña colada. He preferred single malt scotch, but this was in memory of what had led to the greatest turnaround of his life.

"Roger? Roger Milford? Is that really you? What are you doing here in Cancun?"

He looked up. "Hi, Charlie. You do know, don't you, that anyone with a passport can come here?"

Charlie Singleton pulled up a chair. "I imagine you're celebrating. I hear your numbers are through the roof."

"Well, I'm celebrating, all right. I'm down with a group of employees who have had a wonderful year."

"Really? You're with your employees. I wouldn't have expected that from you."

"That was the old Roger, the one who'd lost the handle on his enthusiasm for a job well done. I brought my wife along, too. It's the second honeymoon we never had."

"Good heavens. Well, I suppose you can't tell me how you did whatever you did for one of the great transformation stories of the industry. If everyone knew, it would level the playing field."

"I can and will tell you. Not everyone's up to what it takes, but no one's arguing with the results. It's going to have to wait until a time over dinner, though. Here come my vacation mates. I promised to join them in a game of pool volleyball."

"You, sporting about with your employees? I have seen something truly unique now."

Roger winked at Charlie as he rose and headed for the pool. "You have indeed, Charlie. Something quite unique, and good."

Index

W–Z

FINANCIAL TIMES

In an increasingly competitive world, it is quality
of thinking that gives an edge—an idea that opens new
doors, a technique that solves a problem, or an insight
that simply helps make sense of it all.

We work with leading authors in the various arenas
of business and finance to bring cutting-edge thinking
and best-learning practices to a global market.

It is our goal to create world-class print publications
and electronic products that give readers
knowledge and understanding that can then be
applied, whether studying or at work.

To find out more about our business
products, you can visit us at www.ftpress.com.

Explore More Ways to Live a *Thank God It's Monday*™ Life...

Congratulations! If you apply the lessons and strategies you've discovered in this book, you'll be well on your way to leading a life free from energy-sucking vampires. Keep the journey going with these great recommended resources.

Subscribe to the *Thank God It's Monday* E-Zine.

Continue to develop the principles of TGIM by signing up for the free TGIM e-zine filled with practical advice, tongue-in-cheek quips, and easy-to-implement tips.

Sign-up today at **www.ThankGoditsMonday.com**.

Bonus TGIM Audio Messages, Too!

Start off each Monday fired-up and ready to create a breakthrough by listening to a weekly *TGIM Audio Message*. Our magical TGIM fairy will deliver enlightening quick tips and insights to your in-box each week for six weeks. How do you get this amazing gift? Simple. Just sign up for the free TGIM e-zine at **www.ThankGoditsMonday.com**.

Bring Roxanne Emmerich to Your Company to Develop Your Own *Thank God It's Monday* Culture!

Roxanne Emmerich is one of today's most in-demand transformation agents in business services. She has repeatedly created immediate and massive improvement in workplace productivity through culture change, organizational development, and employee motivation for leading businesses across the country. Watch her speaker demo video at **www.RoxanneEmmerich.com**.

To bring Roxanne Emmerich to your company, email **Culture.Shift@ThankGoditsMonday.com** or call 952-820-0360.

Volume Purchases Available.

Give a copy of the *Thank God It's Monday!* book to all of your employees or clients. Good news! This book is available for bulk volume discounts. Go ahead—get a copy for everyone you care about! To inquire about volume discount pricing for ten or more copies, please send a note to **TGIM@ThankGoditsMonday.com** or call 952-820-0360.